ACCLAIM FOR

TAKE THIS JOB AND SELL IT!

! "Through Richard Mackie's expert efforts...
the business of finding competent personnel has become infinitely easier and more
enjoyable."

> — Tony Chadwick, Regional Director, Northern Division,
> Application Design and Systems, Inc.

! "I urge you to examine this very thorough, excellent resource by a leader in the field."

> — *Cornucopia, Ideas for Better Living*

! "We're pleased with the recruitment. Richard Mackie deserves compliments for his
tenacity and resourcefulness."

> — Richard J. Bradshaw, Executive Vice President, Landsing Corp.

! "Mackie challenges some of the methods currently in use. This is a valuable
addition to the business opportunity seeker's library by one of the leading
practitioners."

> — *HOO (Home Office Opportunities)*

TAKE THIS JOB AND SELL IT!

THE RECRUITER'S HANDBOOK

Richard Mackie

QED Press
Fort Bragg, California

Take This Job and Sell It! The Recruiter's Handbook
Copyright ©1994, 2007 by Richard Mackie

QED PRESS
155 Cypress Street, Fort Bragg, CA 95437
(707) 964-9520   Fax (707) 964-7531
www.qedpress.com

Library of Congress Cataloging-in-Publication Data

Mackie, Richard, 1933-
    Take this job and sell it! : the recruiter's handbook / Richard Mackie.-- 2nd ed.
        p. cm.
    Includes index.
    ISBN-13: 978-0-936609-42-3 (pbk. : alk. paper)
    1. Employees--Recruiting--Vocational guidance--Handbooks, manuals, etc. 2. Executives--Recruiting--Handbooks, manuals, etc. I. Title.
    HF5549.5.R44M29 2006
        658.3'111--dc22   2006008343

Printed in the U.S.A.
Second edition

1 3 5 7 9 8 6 4 2

DEDICATION

In our journey through life we meet hundreds of people who play a role in how our life is played out. I am indebted to all those who had an impact on my life, not just through acquaintance, but through their art, literature and music. I had a patient older brother and exceptional parents who made my early life special and provided a great opportunity to love and to learn. For the production of this book, I owe a debt of gratitude to Perry White & Associates for involving me in the business of recruiting and for allowing me to begin teaching the "art" of recruiting. Special thanks are also due Newton Associates for helping me mature as a recruiter and for allowing me to train all their recruiters while I continued to refine and improve my techniques. However, I am most indebted to my wife Jean who supported me when I decided to become a recruiter and who encouraged me to write this book. There is no greater motivation for success than support and encouragement from one's spouse.

CONTENTS

INTRODUCTION

THERE IS NO WAY TO
MAKE PEOPLE LIKE
CHANGE. YOU CAN ONLY
MAKE THEM FEEL LESS
THREATENED BY IT.

— FREDERICK O.R. HAYES

A quiet revolution is changing the job market in America. Traditional means of conducting business are no longer cost-effective to employers or satisfying to employees. Job security and company loyalty are things of the past, and the average worker can expect to change jobs many times during his lifetime. Social concerns are also influencing business decisions, and many people would like to find ways to earn a satisfactory living while working at home.

» The physical and mental stress of battling freeway traffic every morning and evening has made many employees who endure this daily ritual desperate for alternatives that are closer to home.

» Many working parents want to spend more time with their children.

» The availability and high cost of quality child care has forced some families to reconsider career options.

» Direct and indirect costs of employment are forcing companies to downsize and making mid-level workers aware of the need to take control of their careers.

In the larger metropolitan areas, most workers spend an hour or two, day after day, week after week, commuting to work. Not only does this steal time from their families and from their decreasing leisure time, hundreds of cities choke beneath an unhealthy cloud of toxic emissions as commuters struggle along the freeways that lie between home and work. Our roads need repair, but municipalities haven't the money to fix them. The job market is tight, so employees requesting flex time, salary increases, or permission to work at home may find themselves on the unemployment line rather than stuck in traffic. Something has to change. Our current employment practices are unhealthy for us as individuals and as a society.

Three Problems
Afflicting Most Home Businesses

Unfortunately, most of the ways that people have come up with to earn money while working at home do not provide enough income to allow them to quit their current position. Books that propose home business opportunities provide neither the capital nor the training necessary to turn the ideas into successful money-making ventures.

Take This Job and Sell It! overcomes three major problems that have made it so difficult to start and run a profitable home business.

1. Recruiting is a lucrative business that can be run out of your home very effectively. Currently, the *average* independent recruiter earns about $100,000 per year, while the *exceptional recruiter* earns in excess of $200,000 per year. Even an uninspired recruiter, working independently, should make $50,000 or $60,000 per year. Here is a business that can be run out of your home and still provide you with a livable income.

2. Recruiting requires very little in the way of capital investment. All you really need is a telephone, some business stationery, and business clothes for the infrequent interviews you'll want to conduct.

3. There is a great deal of difference between *understanding* that recruiting is a lucrative business and *being* a successful recruiter, which is why *Take This Job and Sell It!* will teach you everything you need to know to make you a success. Designed not only to help you completely understand the business of recruiting, this book will take you through the step-by-step process you must follow to become a successful recruiter.

I've done it for more than ten years, recruiting computer programmers for some of the best mid-sized companies in America. I've tried dozens of methods, tested them, and I know how recruiting works! For a number of years I've taught courses in recruiting, and *Take This Job and Sell It!* contains the very best these training courses have to offer. You can make a very good living if you approach recruiting with the proper attitude. However, there's no free lunch here. Recruiting requires hard work, not in the sense of physical labor, but in terms of communication skills and self-discipline. You must be willing to pick up a telephone and talk with strangers. And you must be able to handle rejection.

In common with all courses and books designed to help you become successful, *Take This Job and Sell It!* requires a willingness to face rejection in order to experience success. You'll learn to anticipate rejection and treat it as a form of success. (If only one out of five contacts are successful, then four rejections are a necessary part of success.) To be a successful recruiter, you'll learn to regard rejection as something that takes you one step closer to a successful relationship.

Turning a rejection (I call them objections) into a profitable venture is discussed in detail in *Take This Job and Sell It!* I'll show you how to turn objections into long term relationships that will bring you a good deal of business.

HEAD HUNTERS VS RECRUITERS

Many people confuse recruiting with "head hunting," a phrase that grabs headlines. Head hunting, however, is generally reserved for those few agencies that undertake searches for very high ranking company officials whose salaries approach the million dollar mark. Less than 2% of those in the recruiting business involve themselves in head hunting. For instance, when Apple Computer was looking for a new Chief Executive Officer, the Board of Directors provided the head hunter with the names of four people. It was up to the head hunter to entice one of the four people on the list to become Apple's new C.E.O.

In order to carry out such an assignment, a head hunter must spend a good deal of money wining and dining the candidates, flying them around the country and putting them up in expensive hotels. It is rumored that the recruiting agency that lured John Scully away from Pepsi Cola was paid nearly $300,000. Whatever the fee, the agency spent a good deal of time and money earning it. Head hunting is a high risk, high profit business that's not for the average recruiter, and I won't spend much time on it in this book. You don't have to undertake risky activities to make a sizable income in the recruiting business.

So, what is it that recruiters do? A recruiter is an expert in the hiring process, someone who understands what an employer needs and what a prospective employee has to offer. In simple terms, recruiters help their clients fill positions with an annual salary in the $20,000 to $100,000 range. They find candidates in nearby communities, so no one has to travel, be entertained or be put up in hotels. The average recruiter operates where expenses and risks are minimal and enjoys a good deal of independence while earning a very respectable income. However, with this success comes a price. You must be willing to take the time to learn the business thoroughly. And that's where *Take This Job and Sell It!* comes in. Bear with me and I'll teach you what recruiting is all about and provide you with the basic training you need to become successful. If you study your lessons well, you'll do well financially. You'll say good-bye to your old job and to commuting, say hello to your family, and enjoy every aspect of your new career.

Are you ready? Then, let's start recruiting!

CHAPTER 1

THE CLIENT, THE AGENCY, AND THE INDEPENDENT RECRUITER

SUCCESS OCCURS WHEN OPPORTUNITY MEETS PREPARATION.

Before getting into the way recruiting works, study the terms in the glossary in the back of the book. This will eliminate confusion and expedite communication. Refer to the glossary whenever you're unsure of the meaning of one of the terms used in this book.

In the recruiting business, the client always pays the fee. There are businesses where the candidate pays the fee, but these are generally called personnel or employment agencies. Although they might try to convince a potential client otherwise, those who work in personnel agencies are not recruiters and often earn less than $25,000 a year. They are more accurately telemarketers with no special skills or training in the fine art of recruiting.

Nor is a person who works for a recruitment agency where the client always pays the fee necessarily a recruiter. People who work in recruitment agencies usually have no idea how to recruit, although this is not generally their fault. The agency they work for may not *want* to train them, or may not be *able* to train them to become recruiters.

Recruiting is not taught in school. The only place you are likely to learn the trade is in a recruitment agency. At one time, these agencies did make an effort to train their employees to become true recruiters. I alone trained at least forty or fifty recruiters for various companies. Some companies soon learned this could be counter-productive.

WHY GOOD RECRUITERS ARE SCARCE

Recruiters are not paid salaries by the companies they work for. Instead they are paid a commission on the fees they generate. Recruiters generally receive 40% to 50% of the fees they bring in, and the recruitment agency keeps the rest. The average recruiter will generate between $120,000 and $150,000 in fees each year, with between $60,000 and 75,000, retained by the agency to cover expenses and keep the owner's yacht well-stocked with Mumm's. Good recruiters, those who account for $300,000 in fees, must still fork over 50% of the fees earned, although they will be allowed to keep $150,000 a year.

Smart recruiters realize that it's not necessary to maintain a $5,000 per month office on the twentieth floor of the Embarcadero Building in the San Francisco Financial District. They also realize that, contrary to popular belief, the average monthly phone bill for a recruiter is around $250 or $300, not the $2,500

or $3,000 they had imagined. They soon figure out that they are paying their agency somewhere between $5,000 and $7,000 a month for $300 to $500 worth of support. Therefore, soon after they are fully trained, they go out on their own and start to compete with the recruiting company that trained them.

This creates a double loss for the agency:

» They lose the income the trained recruiters generated through the fees that were collected from their clients.

» They lose business because recruiters inevitably take many clients with them when they set up their own shop.

This has created such a problem that some recruitment agencies no longer use well-trained recruiters, leaving the door wide open for the well-trained few who go into the business of recruiting on their own.

Many client companies have become aware that they can get better results working with a good, independent recruiter. The service is quicker, and hiring managers aren't hassled by working with glorified telemarketers. Clients also get a break financially, since they don't have to pay for an agency's overhead in a high rent district.

In the chapters that follow, I'm going to teach you how to become a good, successful, professional recruiter and how to set up your own recruiting business at home or in a small office, but first a word of caution.

WARNING: There are only a few ways to succeed in this business and a thousand ways to fail. Most people fail because the business looks so easy that they follow the path of least resistance and end up functioning like an agency.

As an independent recruiter, you cannot compete effectively if you work like an agency. Not unless you only want to make the $20,000 to $25,000 per year that an agency employee makes.

THE RECRUITMENT AGENCY

There is a subtle but very important difference between what is taught in this book and what takes place in many recruitment agencies. The difference is both philosophical and functional.

Most recruitment agencies these days are little more than resumé mills. Because their employees are not well trained, they must deal with paper and deal in volume. In principal, their goal is to gather as many resumés as possible and get them in front of as many companies as possible. They hope that one of the companies where they have spread their good cheer will find a resumé they like and will agree to pay a fee if the company ends up hiring the person behind the resumé.

This system seldom *works* but is always *mandatory* when working with large companies. These companies are layered with bureaucratic middle management, and the human resources department has had the opportunity to build a dynasty to which other department managers must pay homage. A department manager who tries to circumvent the system for hiring established by human resources had better start looking for employment elsewhere. If the manager isn't fired outright, he or she can, at the very least, expect to be severely admonished. Regardless of how inefficient the human resources department is in finding candidates to fill open positions, the other departments must suffer through the system it established. Because human resources has complete control over the hiring process, it wields great power over other departments. It also wields great power over recruitment agencies vying for the company's business. It's been my experience that a large company turns sixty or seventy positions a year over to recruiting agencies. This amounts to over $500,000 in business, enough to make the manager/owner of any recruiting agency drool a little.

THE HUMAN RESOURCES DEPARTMENT

In order to get any business from one of these large companies, you must get on its human resource list. To get on that list, the manager/owner of the recruitment agency must entertain the client company's Director of Human Resources. This entertainment can mean something as innocuous as a free lunch or something as elaborate as a week's vacation in Mexico City. I once asked the manager of the computer department at one of these big companies how to get on their human resource list. He didn't know for sure, but he could tell me that the human resource manager frequently bragged that he never had to buy his own lunch or dinner.

In exchange, for this "entertainment," the manager of the human resource department will make sure that the recruitment agency is included on the list. Agencies on the list will be notified when the client company has an opening that they need help in filling. Depending on the integrity of the human resources manager, the list may contain as few as five recruiting agencies or as many as twenty.

In either event, when the human resources department signals that it needs help in filling a position, employees at somewhere between five and twenty agencies spring into action.

HOW HIRING WORKS AND WHY IT FAILS

Here's a scenario that portrays how the hiring process functions when the relationship between a recruitment agency and the client company is directed by the human resources department. Let's assume that the accounting manager in the client company wants to hire a cost accountant.

Once the cost-accounting position is officially approved, the accounting manager requests that human resources begin the search. Accompanying the request will be a brief description of what the employee will be doing and what type of person is needed to carry out these functions. The human resources department has several options available for finding a satisfactory cost accountant. It may:

» post a notice internally (within the company), to see if anyone already working for the company is interested in and qualified for the position;

» offer the company's employees a reward for finding a cost accountant (much like a bounty system);

» run an advertisement in one or more newspapers.

Failing to find a suitable candidate, the personnel department may turn to its list of recruitment agencies. These pursuits may occur at once or they may happen one after another.

At Wonderwidgets Inc., a notice is posted internally for one week. When nothing happens, the company's employees are offered a bonus for finding a cost accountant. At the same time, an advertisement is placed in the newspaper and run for three weeks. When none of these methods produce a satisfactory candidate, the project is assigned to the list of recruitment agencies approved by the human resources department. Under these circumstances, the agencies may get the position four or five weeks after the accounting manager at Wonderwidgets Inc. sent personnel the original requisition. With so much time having already elapsed, you would think there would be some sense of urgency to hire a cost accountant. However, when the recruitment agencies take on the assignment, the process continues at the same leisurely pace, even though somewhere between five and twenty recruitment agencies with somewhere between twenty and 100 employees are now trying to grab the golden ring, the recruitment fee.

To this point, communications between the human resources department and the recruitment agencies have been minimal. No one has a firm understanding of the job description or of the ideal cost accountant. Under the circumstances, it is natural for the agencies to submit resumés from every candidate who even remotely fits the imagined position. Agencies consider it far better to submit a bunch of resumés that don't match than to miss one that does. After all, the one who finds the right candidate will get a big fee.

Within a few days, things go from famine to frenzy at a desk in Wonderwidgets Inc.'s personnel office, now stacked floor to ceiling with resumés from various agencies. Some poor clerk sits at that desk and frantically tries to match the resumés with the job description and candidate profile provided by the hiring manager, now desperate to find a decent cost accountant. If the clerk finds any that seem to match, it's turned over to the hiring manager for evaluation.

Now the clerk may have absolutely no idea what a cost accountant is or what one does. So the match is made by looking for buzz words on the resumés. If a resumé has a lot of the right buzz words, it will reach the hiring manager. If the resumé has only a few of the right buzz words, the hiring manager will never see it.

Smart recruitment agencies understand this, so to get most of their candidate resumés before the hiring manager they just need to make sure that lots of the right buzz words show up in the right places on the resumés. Agencies therefore encourage candidates to tailor their resumés to fit the position. At Wonderwidgets Inc. one obvious buzz word for the candidate's last position is the title "cost accountant." It makes little difference whether the candidate actually functioned as a cost accountant. The clerk sorting out the resumés will never know the difference. Other buzz words might include knowledge of certain software packages and certain cost accounting systems.

Once the promising resumés reach the hiring manager's desk, the manager must abandon his normal responsibilities in order to read each of them. Since many of the resumés have most likely been rewritten so as to get passed on by the personnel clerk, the hiring manager will have to read a great many resumés. Reading resumés is not the best way to utilize the time of a $60,000 per year accounting manager.

From the massive pile, the hiring manager may spot one or two resumés that hold some promise. These candidates seem to have most of the experience and skills the accounting manager is looking for in a cost accountant. Likely candidates are identified by the hiring manager and sent back to human resources so arrangements can be made for an interview between the hiring manager and the candidate. Since the hiring manager has many other pressing duties to take care of, it often takes a week or longer to read all the resumés. It has now been more than five weeks since the hiring manager at Wonderwidgets Inc. first asked human resources to start a search.

Once the hiring manager tells personnel who is to be interviewed, human resources must then contact the recruiting agency and inform the agency that Wonderwidgets Inc. wants to see Candidate X. A whole new can of worms now gets opened.

A scrupulous recruitment agency with good employees will have submitted only the resumés of those candidates they have contacted about the position. The agency will have obtained the candidates' permission to submit their resumés to the client company. This, however, takes time and money, two commodities that are in short supply in many agencies. Therefore, many agencies think nothing of submitting *all* the resumés that they think might fit the position. Some of these resumés may be several years old. An agency may not have talked to a candidate for a year, maybe longer. Many candidates will have moved and can no longer be located. Other candidates will have accepted other positions and have no interest in interviewing for this position. To cover themselves, the agency has little choice but to lie. It will advise human resources that Wonderwidgets Inc. took too long in selecting candidates and that Candidate X was forced to accept a position with another company.

Should the desired candidate, by some quirk of good fortune, be available and interested in the position, setting up an interview can be a three-ring circus, especially if the hiring manager is very busy and the candidate is still working. Here's a typical scenario:

TIME LINE

Day One

Agency to Human Resources Department: "Candidate Smith can interview at eight in the morning on Thursday or on Friday after five in the afternoon."

Human Resources Department to Agency: "I'll check with the hiring manager and get back to you if the times are okay with him."

Day Two

Human Resources Department to Agency: "The manager will not be available either of those times. He will be out of town Friday and all of next week."

Agency to Human Resources Department: "Okay. Well, I know that Candidate Smith can't come in any other time this week. I'll contact you a week from Monday when the

manager is back in town. I'll check with Candidate Smith about possible times during that week."

Day Eleven

Well, you get the picture.

If the human resources department and the agency finally connect hiring manager and candidate, there is still not much of a chance that the candidate will be hired. All the critical parts of the hiring process are missing. You will learn all about these parts in subsequent chapters.

After seven or eight weeks, the hiring manager does not yet have a cost accountant and the agency has not yet earned a placement fee. This process is typical of what goes on between most client companies and the recruiting agencies they work with. It is also a process that you must avoid at all costs, because:

» Recruiting fees are based on the annual salary of the candidate placed with the client company. Most agencies claim they charge 30% of the candidate's annual salary as a fee. For instance, if the candidate's annual salary is $40,000, the fee would be 30% or $12,000. Some agencies *say* they charge as much as 35%; however, large companies with domineering human resource departments set their own fees, usually at around 15% or 20%. Take it or leave it. This means you've lost almost one half your fee before you start.

» You will be competing with fifteen or twenty other agencies that collectively may have as many as fifty or 100 employees working on the assignment.

» Since you have not had the opportunity to discuss what kind of person the hiring manager is looking for, your chances of finding the right candidate are slim.

» You haven't had the opportunity to put all the pieces of the hiring puzzle together. Even if your candidate is selected by the hiring manager, chances are not good that he or she will start to work and you will collect the fee.

» Because of these problems and others we will discuss later, your chances of making a placement and earning a fee are about one in sixty. This means that out of every sixty search assignments you get, you will make only one placement and collect only one fee.

THE INDEPENDENT RECRUITER

By way of contrast, the *average* independent recruiter who learns the trade will collect fees on one out of every two or, at worst, one out of every three search assignments. Good recruiters will collect a fee on four out of every five search assignments they accept. Obviously, this is better than collecting one fee for every sixty search assignments. The fees a trained recruiter collects will also be substantially larger.

Obviously, you'd rather collect a $10,000 fee on half your search assignments than a $6,500 fee on one out of every sixty search assignments you accept. Why, you'd only need to work on twenty-four assignments per year to pocket $120,000, compared to the untrained person who would need to work on about 720 search assignments to collect $78,000 in fees. Getting twenty-four search assignments a year is relatively easy. Getting 720 is impossible. Training may be a pain, but it is well worth undertaking.

Assuming, then, that you would rather be a trained recruiter than a recruitment agency, the following rules must be diligently followed. Read them over and over until they become part of your work habits. Never forget them. Each time you do it could cost you a $10,000 fee.

ELEVEN ESSENTIAL RULES
FOR INDEPENDENT RECRUITERS

1. You are an expert in the hiring process, *not* in an area of specialization. Just because you recruit accountants doesn't mean you are an accountant. If you sell a client on the idea that you are the right recruiter for a search because you are knowledgeable in accounting, your success is going to be negatively impacted. The idea you must sell to your client is that you are an expert in the hiring process. You know how to get the right candidate, get that person on the client company's payroll in record time, and do it with a minimum of hassle. *Because* of your specialization in an area, you will become familiar with the jargon in that field, and this will make it easier for you and the hiring manager to discuss what goes on in an accounting department. However, it is not necessary to know these things in order to become an effective recruiter.

2. Hiring managers are *not* experts in the hiring process. They may believe they are because they have been poorly trained by human resources and/or recruiting agencies. The average manager hires only four or five employees in his or her entire career. You, on the other hand, will be involved in a great many hirings, and you are specially trained in this process. Working together, you and the hiring manager can utilize each other's expertise to great advantage.

3. Plan your day, your week and your month ahead of time. Set your goals for the month, then plan your daily and weekly activities around these goals. Many good recruiters set financial goals for themselves for the month and the year, then plan their activities around how they will meet their financial goals. In this book you will find some formulas you can use to establish and meet your monthly and annual financial goals. This is the hardest part of recruiting. Sticking to goals is difficult, particularly if you are working alone at home. It takes a lot of self discipline, especially when you could be watching television or baking cookies. Recruiters who don't have a lot of self discipline are better off renting a small office away from home where there are no distractions.

4. Work only with small to medium size companies. Companies with earnings of over $500 million a year are far too big and bureaucratic to deal with effectively. Leave them to the recruitment agencies. You will lose nothing by sticking to smaller companies since 80% of all open positions will be found there. You will be constantly tempted to pursue search assignments for big companies. Do not yield to the temptation.

5. Specialize. Find a discipline in which you like to work and specialize in that area. Some people love computers and specialize in recruiting computer programmers; oth-

ers love accounting and finance and recruit people in that area. Select an area where you will enjoy talking with people in that profession. Nothing is worse than talking all day with people about a subject you have no interest in. We will delve more into selecting an area of specialization later in this chapter.

6. Don't be tempted to work outside your area of specialization. Inevitably, one of your client companies will ask you to search for someone outside your chosen field. Your mental cash register will immediately ring up a $12,000 fee. Ignore the chime. You will find yourself spending weeks on the position and chances are slim to none that you will be able to fill it. Meantime, you will be missing opportunities in your area of specialization. If you want to provide full service to your clients, accept the search but don't do it yourself. Split the search with a recruiter who specializes in placing candidates in that other area of specialization. Splitting a $12,000 fee is not bad considering the other recruiter is going to do the work. Most recruiters will do 50/50 splits on these assignments. Get to know the independent recruiters in your area and what they specialize in, so you can take advantage of splits. They may have some for you to work on as well. (Note that recruitment agencies and people working for them won't do splits, since the agency and the person working on the assignment would have to split their half of the fee a second time.)

7. Develop relationships. Be pleasant, easy and efficient. At first, hiring managers may resist working with you the way I will train you to work. However, once they have worked with you, they will come back again and again. This makes your business much easier. Recruitment agency methods do not allow for the development of relationships with hiring managers.

8. Learn to say no. As you prospect for search assignments, you will run across many situations where you will be asked to do a search on terms other than your own. Don't accept the assignment. This is difficult, but it is essential. The further you move away from the methods taught here, the closer you move toward becoming a recruitment agency, and the lower your success rate will be. Your placement rate will move from one placement for every two search assignments to one placement for every sixty search assignments. Do your best to sell a potential client on working your way. If you can't, don't be afraid to walk away from the assignment. Your time will be better spent finding assignments where you can be most effective.

9. Be kind to all your candidates, even the pesky ones. They may turn out to be hiring managers one day. One candidate I placed twice is now a manager. He has hired four people through me, making six placements from one individual. Even if the pesky ones are not placed and will never be managers, they can always be good sources of other candidates or search assignments. Don't underestimate their value.

10. Be aware of the various employment laws. While employment laws will not affect you directly, you need to be certain that a client isn't asking you to break the law. If a company tells you it only wants to see candidates of a particular race, sex or age, don't accept the assignment. The client is asking

you to discriminate, and this is against the law. Be aware that the Labor Department will occasionally send a ringer to an employment agency to see if they are discriminating on behalf of a client. Let clients do the discriminating if they are looking for someone special. (This happens on occasion when a company tries to meet its quota of minority hirings.)

11. Keep reviewing these rules until you understand each of them. Then review them again until you understand why each one is essential to your success.

SELECTING YOUR AREA OF SPECIALIZATION

Recruiters can chose from many different professions in selecting their specialized area of recruiting. Each profession demands a slightly different approach. Some recruiters enjoy working with software engineers, but they are difficult to find and to recruit. Client companies will climb all over recruiters who can find certain kinds of software engineers, so marketing for search assignments is a relatively simple task. Finding candidates, on the other hand, can be arduous. Some recruiters would rather market than recruit and will select a profession where the candidates are fairly easy to come by but good search assignments are more difficult to find. Once you have been in business for a while, you will begin to discover whether you prefer recruiting or marketing, and this may make a difference in the type of professional you decide to work with. It is not unusual for a recruiter to change his or her area of specialization. Obviously, the best recruiters are those

who enjoy recruiting *and* marketing and do both well.

Most clients and many recruiters assume that a recruiter's primary function is to find candidates for positions that are difficult to fill. If you believe this, look at Rule #1 once again. Both you and the client company need to understand that you are there for your expertise in the hiring process. If recruiters' only function were to locate hard-to-find candidates, they would all specialize in recruiting software engineers with expertise in designing UNIX kernels or other specialized engineers that virtually every computer manufacturer in the world would like on its staff and would pay dearly to get. However, few recruiters work in these highly specialized areas and manage to do extremely well financially. There just aren't enough candidates.

Some professions require more training and/or education than others. As a rule, the more training and education a profession requires, the higher a salary that profession will command. This may be an important consideration, since the fee you collect for completing a search assignment is usually based on the candidate's salary. For instance, if you have agreed to a 25% fee and the candidate's salary is $50,000 a year, your fee will be $12,500. However, if the candidate's salary is $30,000 a year, your fee will be only $7,500. The most highly-paid professionals are usually more difficult to recruit, so you may fill fewer positions.

Here are three categories of professions. Pick the one you think you would enjoy working with and learning about. If you have an unyielding love for marketing and hate recruiting, or vise versa, then choosing the market-rich category becomes more important.

Note: Within each category is a partial list intended to give you some idea of what there is to chose from. There are hundreds of other professions you might be interested in working with. Do not, however, select a profession that requires little or no education or special training. Also, avoid professions that are labor intensive or unionized. Few companies will hire a recruiter to fill positions that are not professional in nature or are highly unionized. Also, avoid governmental professions. Civil Service agencies are impossible to work with.

Category A

**Professions that require
more recruiting than marketing**

- » Software engineers (almost any kind)
- » Certain computer professionals (*i.e.,* systems programmers)
- » Certain accounting people (*i.e.,* cost accountants, MIS auditors)
- » Certain lawyers in specialized areas.
- » Most physicians, particularly physician specialists.
- » Certain nurse specialists.
- » Most research scientists
- » Certain sales and marketing professionals

Category B

**Professions that require equal amounts
of marketing and recruiting**

- » Most computer professionals
- » Most accounting professionals
- » Hardware engineers
- » Process engineers
- » Other medical personnel
- » Nurses
- » Dentists
- » Most sales and marketing professionals

Category C

**Professions that require
more marketing than recruiting**

- » Secretarial/clerical staff with special computer skills
- » Bookkeepers with special computer skills
- » Most middle management positions (for almost any profession)
- » Dental/medical assistants
- » General sales personnel

EVALUATING A SEARCH ASSIGNMENT

Everyone wants to work on a search assignment where the odds of filling the position are four out of five (80%). However, in order to do this, you need to be able to assess your chances of filling the position. Basically, there are three factors that determine what your chances are of filling a given position:

1. The number of other recruiters working on filling the position

2. The control you have over the hiring process

3. The availability of candidates

In order to have an 80% chance of filling the position you must have:

1. an exclusive on the position (no other recruiters working on it);

2. total control of the hiring process; and

3. a strong database of candidates who will fit the position.

The reason the odds are 80% and not 100% is because not all positions get filled. The company may suddenly institute a hiring freeze, or decide to eliminate the position, or fill the position with an internal candidate. If none of these things ever happened, your chances of filling the position would be 100%, because you have complete control over who fills the position. However, they do happen, and they need to be taken into account when you are setting up your plans for reaching your financial goals.

Although you will always strive to get a search assignment with an 80% probability of filling, this is not always possible. Therefore, you need to be able to assess your likelihood of filling search assignments where you do not have an exclusive, or where you do not have complete control of the hiring process, or where you have a limited number of candidates in your database.

To look at it another way, if you were working on an assignment where your only involvement in the search process is to send resumés to personnel (as most recruitment agencies do), then your chances of filling that position are one in sixty (less than 2%).

Be wary of falling into a state of complacency. If your goal is one placement per month and you have five search assignments, it is easy to lull yourself into believing that you have several placements in the bag. However, when the search assignments are examined carefully, you may find that they are not much different from those that the recruitment agencies work on. In reality, there is only a 10% chance (2% multiplied by five assignments = 10%) that you will make a placement that month. Here are some hints on how to evaluate your chances of filling search assignments. These will have more meaning when you have finished this book and have learned what it means to have an exclusive (area of competition), to have control of the hiring process (area of control), and to have a strong database of candidates (area of database). Let's look at each of these areas and outline the best to worst situations.

AREA OF COMPETITION

Best

A) You have an exclusive. Client is using no other recruiters, and client is not running ads in the newspaper or offering employees hiring bonuses.

B) You have an exclusive. Client is using no other recruiters but client is running an ad and/or offering hiring bonuses.

C) Client is using other recruiters.

D) Client is using other recruiters and is running ads, etc.

Worst

AREA OF CONTROL

Best

A) You are working with the hiring manager and have complete authority in determining who will be interviewed. You also determine when and where the interviews will take place.

B) You are working with the hiring manager and have complete authority in determining who will be interviewed.

C) You are working in conjunction with the hiring manager in deciding who will be interviewed.

D) You are working with the hiring manager, but he or she makes an independent determination as to who will be interviewed.

E) You have contact with the hiring manager but must work through human resources.

F) You have no contact with the hiring manager. Your only communications is with human resources.

G) You have no contact with the hiring manager and your only means of communications about the position is sending a resumé to human resources.

Worst

AREA OF DATABASE

Best

A) The position is a perfect fit with your area of specialization and you have a large database of individuals eager to move to a new position.

B) The position is in your area of specialization and you have a fair number of candidates who could fill the position.

C) The position is in your area of specialization and, while you have a limited number of candidates, you can get easy referrals.

D) The position is closely related to your area of specialization and people in your database should be able to provide you with referrals.

E) The position has no relation to your database and you have to start from scratch. (This is a great time to offer a split with a recruiter who does specialize in this profession.)

Worst

In all, there are 140 possible combinations of the above, and while I am not going to analyze every possible combination, by the time you finish this book and gained a little experience, you should be able to return to this section and determine your chance of success within a few percentage points. Obviously, if the search assignment rates an "A" in each category, your chances of filling the position are at least 80%.

If you are in competition with other recruiters but have complete control of the hiring process ("A" in Control) and the position is in your area of expertise ("A" or "B" in database) you should still have about a 60% to 70% chance of filling the position. This is because you will control who is being interviewed and can eliminate your competitors' candidates.

On the other hand, if you have an exclusive but no control over the hiring process, or if the position is out of your area of expertise, your chances of filling the position will be about 20% or 25% (one out of four or five). This is because you will not be able to react well or quickly to the assignment and this will allow another recruiter an opportunity to move in and take over.

DEVELOPING A PLAN OF ACTION

To become a good recruiter you'll need to establish some goals and develop a plan of action. If you follow the basic formula demonstrated below, you'll be able to develop a plan to meet your financial goals.

Let's assume that your financial goal for the first year is $100,000. If you work out of your home office, your expenses for the year will be in the neighborhood of $6,000. Therefore, your total income for the year will have to be around $106,000 in order for you to meet your financial goal.

Let's further assume that your area of specialization is accounting. Since the average fee for placing accounting professionals is around $9,000, in order to meet your goal you must place 12 accounting professionals (12 x $9,000 = $108,000). In other words, you must place an average of one person each month.

To place one person a month, you will need to get a certain number of search assignments, recruit a certain number of candidates and set up a certain number of interviews. The number of search assignments you need will depend on the quality of the assignment. If you get a search assignment that can be honestly rated an "A" in every category, you may need only one. However, if your search assignments are rated as "D" or below in all categories, you may need twenty or more search assignments to be sure of making one placement. Most average recruiters will get search assignments that are a combination of "A," "B," and "C" ratings. They generally need four or five search assignments for one placement. A good recruiter who can get three or four "A" search assignments is going to make three or four placements a month. This will be your goal for the second or third year.

Statistics on the recruiting business have been kept for years. Without going into a lot of detail about how these figures were arrived at, I can attest to the following:

If you have six or more candidates interview for a position, you will have an 80% or more chance of filling the position.

If you have four to five candidates interview for a position, you will have about a 50% chance of filling the position.

If you have two to three candidates interview for a position, you will have a 25 to 35% chance of filling the position.

If you have only one candidate interview for a position, you will have a 10 to 15% chance of filling the position.

The number of people you will have interviewing for the position will be determined by how closely the position is aligned to your area of specialization and by how well you have developed your database. Here is the real reason why it is so important to specialize. Your goal is to build a database of people in the profession you have chosen, so that when you find a good search assignment you will be able to react quickly and get as many people as possible interviewed. If the search assignment is not in the area where you have built your candidate database, you will not be able to find the proper candidates before the position is gone or filled in some other manner.

Now that this information is safely tucked away in your mental database, let's put it all together and make it happen for you.

CHAPTER 2

THE SEARCH ASSIGNMENT

IF YOU
ENCOUNTER DIFFICULTY,
DON'T CHANGE
YOUR DECISION TO GO.
CHANGE YOUR DIRECTION
TO GET THERE.

The importance of taking a *proper* search assignment cannot be over-emphasized. The process should be handled carefully and accurately, but I doubt if anyone in a recruiting agency has any idea of how to accept a proper search assignment.

When you receive a search assignment from a client, you must ask all the right questions in sequence. Most likely, the person telling you about the search will make certain assumptions about what information you need. Listen carefully, but be sure you get the information you need when you need it. The search assignment is more than just an agreement between you and the client to undertake a search on the client's behalf. The search assignment is also:

» The first stage in closing the deal (that is, in making sure the client hires your candidate and that the candidate accepts the position).

» Your best opportunity to take control of the hiring process.

» The only way to get the information you

need to make your candidates the top candidates.

» The only way to achieve the credibility you need to set up the kind of agreements you want.

They may not intend to deceive you, but neither the hiring manager nor the clerk from personnel will give you relevant information about the search assignment. You must ferret out this information for yourself

To start with, you will be given the title for the position. For example, you will be told, "We are looking for a Senior Programmer Analyst." Unfortunately, this is an internal title. While other companies may also have senior programmer analysts, there is no universal agreement as to what one is. Each company has its own interpretation of what a programmer analyst does and the salary one should be paid for doing it.

"We want somebody with three to five years experience."

This tells you absolutely nothing. Some programmer analysts have obtained five years worth of experience in just two years. Others have worked for five years and gained just one year of experience (although they did it five times).

Questions about experience are generally followed by a string of buzz words. *"We need someone familiar with an AS-400 computer who can program in RPG III."*

This tells you what buzz words should appear on resumés but tells you little that you need to know to fill the position. All the important things are left out. For instance, what will the candidate be doing? Who will the candidate be working with? What are the candidate's responsibilities? To whom will he or she report?

And yet, people who work in recruiting agencies think that the title, length of experience, and buzz words are sufficient for you to begin a search. That's because they intend to dump a small truckload of resumés on someone's desk. However, that's not nearly good enough for a good recruiter. You may have heard something about what they want, but nothing that you need to do a proper search. You are, after all, not just in the business of doing a search for resumés that have the appropriate buzz words, you are, or soon will be, an expert in the hiring process. In order to carry out your duties effectively on behalf of your clients, you need additional information. You also need to work out several agreements.

On pages 20–22, you'll find a Search Assignment form with the questions you must have answered and the order in which they should be asked. Make a copy of this form before proceeding further, since you will constantly refer to it. Have a copy of this form by your side whenever you take on a search assignment. *(Note: loose forms are also available from the publisher; see the back of the book for ordering information.)* When a client gives you information in a different order than you want it, insert the information wherever it is appropriate, then go back to your orderly sequence. When you reach the question that had previously been considered, reconfirm the information the client gave you earlier.

"Now, as I recall, you suggested that all candidates should be _____ "

Occasionally, someone will wonder why

you *need* all this extra information. After all, the title, buzz words and amount of experience desired was enough for most personnel agencies. Your answer is that you want to offer the client the other 97% of the candidates that the hiring manager would not otherwise have access to. What you mean by this is that the three bits of information offered by the company representative is adequate to attract 3% of the candidates, namely those already actively seeking a job. Generally, these are people who are out of work or in an untenable situation. If this is the only kind of candidate the client is interested in, an advertisement in the newspaper should be sufficient. However, the client should be warned against hiring these high risk candidates. Why you should issue this warning will be explained next chapter.

The other 97% of the candidate base that you have to offer consists of candidates who are not actively looking for a new position. These candidates must be recruited. They are stable candidates whose motive for accepting a new position is that it will be a positive move for the candidate as well as for the client. This is seldom the motive of a candidate who is out of a job or who is in a bad situation. However, in order to recruit candidates from this wonderful 97% of the candidate base, you need much more specific information. Recruiting these candidates will be discussed in depth later.

So, with your Search Assignment outline in hand, let's take the first search assignment.

SEARCH ASSIGNMENT

SA# _____ Date _____ Phone _____

Company _____

Mailing address _____ Zip _____

Street address _____ Zip _____

1. Taken from _____ Title _____

2. Position reports to _____ Title _____

3. Day to day duties _____

_____

4. Part of team? _____ Role? _____

_____

5. Independent responsibilities _____

_____

_____

6. Work with people outside group? _____

Department? _____

Company? _____

7. Special skills needed (verbal, written) _____

_____

8. Preferred skills _____

_____

9. Candidate profile _____

_____

10. Title _____

11. Salary range _____ Top talent _____

12. Negotiation factors _____

_____

_____

13. Interviewing process: First interview _____

Second interview _____ Third interview _____

14. Must hire by _____ 1st int. date _____

2nd int. date _____ Offer date _____

15. Why position open? _____

16. Fee _____ _____ Guarantee _____

17. Benefits ☐ medical ☐ dental ☐ vision ☐ sick leave ☐ holidays _____

☐ vacation ☐ 401K ☐ retirement ☐ profit share ☐ stock ☐ bonus

Other _____

18. Why person might accept position _____

_____

19. Why manager works here _____

_____

20. Department structure _____

_____

_____

21. Promotion/career path _____

_____

_____

22. What company does _____

_____

23. Annual sales _____ No. of employees _____

24. Where co. fits in marketplace _____

25. Company HQ (if not here) _____

26. Scope of market _____

27. Company share of marketplace _____

28. Competitors/hiring sources

COMPANY	CITY	CONTACT	PHONE

29. Would hire candidates from _____

_____

30. Doesn't want candidates from _____

NOTES

INTERPRETING
THE SEARCH ASSIGNMENT FORM

SA# (Search Assignment Number)

Number your search assignments so you can file and reference them. Numbering also lets you know how many search assignments you've accepted in a given period of time.

Date/Phone/Company/Address

Note the date you accepted the search assignment, the telephone number and the company name. Nothing is more frustrating than to discover that you forgot to get the phone number after you've hung up. It's particularly frustrating if the number turns out to be the hiring manager's private line. The number will not be listed, and you can spend hours tracking it down. Get both a street address and mailing address if they are different. The mailing address is needed for all correspondence, and you will soon be providing candidates with the street address as well as directions for getting to the client company when they go for interviews. The remaining information is keyed to the numbers on the Search Assignment form:

1. You need to know from whom you received your information about a search assignment, their title, or what they have to do with the position. Don't assume you are getting the information from the hiring manager. You may find out you are talking to someone who is only indirectly related to hiring for the position. This may be someone within the same department or someone from human resources. Find out early in the game because you must talk with somebody who can set up the necessary agreements. Normally, the only people who can authorize certain agreements

about the hiring process are the hiring manager, the department head or someone with authority in the human resources department.

2. For several reasons, you'll need to know who the successful candidate will report to. The hiring manager may not be this person. The data processing manager may be the hiring manager, but the position may report to and take directions from a project manager. You can learn a lot about the level of the position and how the department is structured by understanding the reporting procedures. If you are asked why this information is necessary, say, "Good candidates want this information before they will consider going for an interview. They need to know that I have talked to you and that you're a nice person to work for." This is a particularly important message for people in human resources to hear. They forget that technical qualifications are only part of the screening process. Personality is also an important factor in the hiring process. Most hiring managers will assume that a candidate is qualified to do the job and will be more concerned with whether they can work with this person for the next two or three years. The candidate is also going to be concerned about the relationship. More about this later.

3. With day to day duties, you begin to sort the wheat from the chaff, or, in this case, the recruiter from the recruitment agency. Here are questions that no one else has asked and that neither the hiring manager nor human resources has thought to discuss with you. And yet Items #3 through #8 are the ones that will determine the type of person needed to fill the position. There are several reasons why Item #3 is important:

» You'll need to find out if your candidates

have carried out these duties before.

» You'll need to know if your candidates have the right skills.

» You'll need to determine if the position's tasks are challenging enough to keep a senior person happy. It is just as bad, or worse, to place someone who is overqualified for a position as it is to place someone who is underqualified for a position.

The hiring manager will be impressed that you are aware and interested in how his or her area functions. The hiring manager will also be impressed that you want to make sure that the candidates you present can carry out the day-to-day duties the position demands.

4. This is another important question that is almost never asked. When you are looking for candidates, you need to know whether they are team players or loners. Do they like to work in a group or do they prefer to work alone? Have they been part of a team previously? Finally, you need to know what role the successful candidate will play on the hiring manager's team. You need this information not only to advise potential candidates but to select the right candidates.

This is one place where resumés fail miserably. Let's assume that the hiring manager wants someone with experience working on an accounts payable system. The resumé may state that the candidate is currently working on an accounts payable system; however, there can be a great deal of difference between two candidates whose resumés sound the same. One candidate may have designed an entire accounts payable system while the other candidate may have been part of a team. The second candidate may have worked on only a small part of the accounts payable system and have no idea how the whole thing fits together, or how other parts of the system work.

The hiring manager is going to be most appreciative and impressed with your knowledge when you point this out. Yet you have demonstrated no knowledge of accounting or data processing or any other technical areas of any profession. What you have demonstrated is that you are an expert in the hiring process. Without really knowing why, the hiring manager will feel that you are an expert in finding the right people for the job. This is because hiring is not decided on the basis of a candidate's technical merits but on his or her ability and interest in doing the job. Everyone understands this, but few can put it into words. Most people fall back on buzz words and position titles.

5. Are there any actions or activities that are exclusively the responsibility of the person filling this position? For instance, are there any weekly or monthly reports that the employee will have sole responsibility for compiling and/or submitting? The answer to this question will provide you with information about the level of written skills needed and whether the company needs a person who can work independently when necessary. When you point out the reason you are asking this question, you will have taken another step toward building the manager's confidence in your ability to find the right candidate. By the time you reach Item #9, you need to have the hiring manager's full confidence because that's when you are going to take charge of the entire hiring process.

6. Here are some important but rarely asked questions. Whom will the employee be contacting during the workday? Will it be just the people in the group or department, or with someone in human resources, shipping, accounting, sales or marketing? What about people outside the company?

All managers want their departments well represented. If the employee will be contacting people outside the department, verbal skills and telephone skills could be important. How the employee gets along with other people also becomes an important issue. Hiring managers understand the relevance of these issues, and their confidence in you continues to grow.

CAUTION: Do not allow the manager to suggest that you discriminate. Be sure to assert that you will be screening for particular skills, not for appearance. You will not discriminate on the basis of race, religion, age, sex, weight or any factor other than skill. If the hiring manager chooses to discriminate, you are helpless to prevent it. Just be sure you are not a party to it.

First Agreements

7. You now know enough about the position so that you and the hiring manager can begin to put together a profile of what sort of person will function well in the position. Continue to take the lead, not by asking questions but by making suggestions. This is the point at which you very quietly and very subtly start to take over the hiring process. Your suggestions should sound something like this:

"From what you've told me, it sounds like you need someone with excellent written communications skills."

You will get an immediate agreement.

"I suspect that someone with good oral communications will also be important."

Another agreement.

"Since this person will be working with both clerical and management personnel within your company, I believe this person should also have demonstrated an ability to work effectively with people at these levels without intimidating people or being intimidated. Don't you agree?"

Another quick agreement.

"Now, it's obvious that this person must have experience on an AS/400 and be able to program in RPG III. Are there any other technical skills that you feel are absolutely mandatory?"

The manager may or may not feel that some other technical skills are mandatory. In either event, you and the manager have reached an agreement as to what characteristics and skills are necessary for a person to function successfully in this position.

This is your first official agreement.

You are going to be the only one who has this understanding with the hiring manager. What's more important, this agreement is a stepping stone to future agreements.

8. There are usually a number of skills that the manager would like candidates to have, but that are not mandatory. In most cases, these additional skills will be of a technical nature. However, on occasion they may be personal in nature. For instance, the manager might like an individual who can speak a particular foreign language. The preferred skills area is sometimes referred to as the manager's "wish list."

"If possible, you'd like the person you

hire to possess drafting skills. Is that right?"

"That would be nice."

This is your second official agreement.

Make sure that none of the skills on the preferred list can take the place of something on the mandatory list. This puts you way ahead of any other recruiters who might be working on the assignment. One of the other recruiters may find a candidate that has most of the preferred skills but whose ability to work with other department managers is suspect. A subtle reminder to the hiring manager will eliminate the competitor's candidate. (Because you know what the manager needs, you can help screen the other candidates later on.)

9. The candidate profile is basically a means of confirming and solidifying the first two agreements. You are taking control.

"Let me make sure I've got everything absolutely right. As a minimum, the candidates must have *(refer to first agreement)*. Is that how you see it?"

Agreement reconfirmed.

"It would also be nice if the candidates had some or all of the following skills *(refer to second agreement)*. Is there anything you can think of that we need to add?"

Second agreement reconfirmed.

10. Now, you and the manager are going to agree on a title for the position. You need to be in charge of this process. Whatever you do, don't ask the hiring manager what the position is called. If you were already told, pretend you didn't hear it or have forgotten it. You will suggest something like the following:

"In other companies I've worked with, they usually call someone working in this position a '_____' or a '_____.' Is this all right with you or did you have some special title in mind for this position."

You don't really care what the position is called, you just want to send a strong but subtle message that not everyone with the same title is doing the same things. They will not have the same skills, abilities or experience. In other words, don't let a person's title influence the decision with regard to whom should be interviewed.

This is a very important point. When looking at resumés, a hiring manager will have nothing much to go on other than a title in deciding whom to interview. You don't want the hiring manager to spend a lot of time interviewing the wrong people. However, this entails fighting against a deep-seated tradition that dictates that screening for candidates should be done by reviewing resumés. This tradition is so well implanted in our hiring culture that it persists in the face of overwhelming evidence that over 80% of the resumés contain blatant lies. However, as long as resumés are viewed as the tool for getting an interview, the resumé is going to contain whatever is necessary to get the candidate in the door. The process encourages lying.

Therefore, for both your sakes, persuade the hiring manager to let you screen the candidates. Go back to candidate profile (Item #9) and quietly review the agreements on the qualifications required of the candidates. There will be nothing in the resumés that will address the most important qualities you and the hiring manager have decided are needed to carry out the functions of the position, such as working as a member of a team, working with people outside the department, oral skills, written skills, etc. These things cannot be discovered by reviewing resumés.

Don't try to take the resumés away from the hiring manager. For most managers, the resumé is a security blanket. They find it almost impossible to interview someone without a resumé in front of them. Your role is just to be sure that the manager only interviews people with the skills essential to the position. Since these skills cannot be found on a resumé, you will screen all the candidates first and submit only the ones where the individual has the appropriate skills.

As a practical matter, you would like to save as much of the hiring manager's time as possible. After all, a lot of other responsibilities are going to be neglected while resumés are sorted, phone calls made and candidates interviewed. Ideally, narrow the field down to four to six finalists. You will then forward the resumés of these four to six candidates to the manager and discuss why each was selected. The manager should have absolutely no problem with that.

This is agreement *number three.*

The manager has now agreed to interview four to six candidates of your choice. (The number will depend upon whether you feel you can find four or six good candidates. If candidates are going to be somewhat difficult to find, you may want to go for just four.) Some recruiters think you should throw one bad candidate into the pot just to make the others look better. I don't agree. The manager is not just interviewing candidates, he or she is also evaluating your judgment in finding good candidates. You want repeat business from this manager. Don't risk messing it up.

More Agreements

11. Almost always, there will already be a salary range assigned to this position. The decision was made at the time the manager drew up the department budget for the year. Generally, there is very little give and take in this area. However, that doesn't mean that the salary set aside for the position is appropriate. If there is a discrepancy in the salary for the position, it is almost always on the low side. Before you spend a lot of time on a search, you need to make sure the salary is in line with the position.

There is, however, a difference between the salary range and the hiring range for the position. The salary range for the position may be $30,000 to $45,000. However, a person is never hired at the top end of the salary range. If they were, employees would never receive a raise in salary until they were promoted. Therefore, companies seldom hire above the middle of the salary range. This means that the hiring range will be about $30,000 to $38,000.

If you are familiar with the salaries people in the profession are receiving, it is appropriate to mention it at this point.

"Based on the skills and experience we've determined the person should have, I suspect we will have to offer a salary in the $40,000 to $42,000 range for top talent."

The manager may balk. Let's say, he or she was only prepared to pay $35,000 to $38,000. If you are unfamiliar with the salaries of people in the profession, you may want to offer the following:

> "That salary doesn't sound quite right for top talent for the position. Let me check it out and get back to you. There is no sense spending a lot of time interviewing candidates who are already making more than you can offer."

The manager will appreciate the gesture. Regardless of whether you know about salaries now or need to check them out later, both you and the manager need to reach an agreement on this point. Once you have the proper information, you can begin negotiating your fourth agreement. If you need to check on the salaries, you can skip to Item #13 and come back to Item #12 (negotiations) at a later time.

12. Should you and the manager differ on salary, negotiate with the hiring manager to raise the top end of the hiring range or to lower the requirements for the position. Almost invariably, the salary itself can't be changed. These negotiations are relatively easy if you keep one thing in mind: it is relatively easy to train people to upgrade their technical skills, but it is almost impossible to train them to change personal skills. In other words, you can teach employees new accounting skills but you'd have difficulty teaching them new verbal skills or how to deal with people. Brought to his or her attention, the hiring manager will agree to this obvious tenet.

Therefore, you and the manager can agree to relax the technical requirements in order to get the best person into the position without raising the salary for the position.

This is agreement number four.

This provides the hiring manager with another great advantage: it is much better to bring in a candidate who is slightly underqualified but bright and eager to learn. Such a candidate will stay longer and be much happier. The only other option is to hire a less desirable candidate with all the technical skills. That candidate may soon leave if there is nothing new to learn or if there are no new challenges.

This provides an additional advantage for you as well. Your competition will fall further and further behind as they scramble for candidates with the right technical qualifications.

The manager will be suspicious of any candidates who have all the skills but are willing to work for this low salary. Although you have never asked for it, you are now close to having an exclusive assignment. You have almost completely shut the door on any other recruiters who may be working on the assignment, particularly those who are searching for candidates based on the three bits of information we talked about at the beginning of this chapter: title, length of experience, and buzz words.

13. One of the biggest mistakes most recruiters make is forgetting to find out who is involved in the interviewing and hiring process. This makes it difficult to coordinate the hiring activities and maintain control of the hiring process. Every company has a different set of rules about who prospective employees must see and deal with. Open up this area of inquiry with a statement such as:

> "I assume that the first interview will be with you. Is there anyone else the candidates will see during the first interview?"

Next you need to know approximately how long the first interview will last. This is vital for several reasons. In the first place, you need to schedule the interviews appropriately. Secondly, the candidates need to know for their own scheduling purposes. Finally, you need to tally the time company employees are going to spend in the interviewing process.

Once you have gleaned everything you can about the first interview, find out who will be involved in the second interview and why. Often, the hiring manager serves primarily as a screener during the first interview . The second interview will frequently be with others involved in the hiring decision. Seldom does a hiring manager make a unilateral decision on whom to hire. If the candidate will be working with people in other departments, these other people are often included in the selection process. You will need this vital information later on when you coach your candidates and close the deal.

14. Once you understand the interviewing process, you are ready to ask the most important question of all: When would you like to have this position filled and the employee on board?

The usual answer is ASAP (as soon as possible). This is not an acceptable answer. You need a target date. If the hiring manager can't give you one, suggest a date. Once you know the target date, you can design a hiring procedure that will have a candidate in the position and working by that date.

THE TYPICAL HIRING PROCESS

Most employment processes, left to their own devices, will take three or four months. With your skills and the cooperation of the hiring manager, this can be reduced to one month. The reason it usually takes so long is that no one stays on top of the hiring process, and it generally moves along this way:

The specifications for the position are determined sometime during the week and an advertisement is placed to run in the Sunday paper. Resumés begin to appear in the mail by Tuesday, slowing to a drizzle by Friday. Without enough good resumés, the ad may be run again the following weekend. Depending on circumstances, the ad can run for a month or longer. I've seen ads run four months. However, for purposes of this scenario, let's assume the ad runs for just one weekend.

By the middle of the following week, 95% of all the resumés that are going to arrive have arrived. A week has gone by, and it is now time to screen the resumés. In some instances, the hiring manager does the screening; in others, human resources handles the initial screening and the hiring manager does a final screening. This can take as little as three days or as long as three weeks. Again, let's assume it was done in the shortest possible time, so we are now a week and a half into the hiring process.

Personnel contacts the selected potential candidates and arranges for them to come in for an interview. Since people are usually at work or out shopping or taking the kids to a little league game, it may take several phone calls over several days to reach the candidate. Finding a time when both the candidate and the hiring manager are able to spend one or more hours in an interview may take several phone calls. It is usually at least three weeks into the hiring process before the first interview takes place.

Now for the worst part of this hiring process. After the first interview, the candidate and the company will have no further contact unless the candidate is eventually invited back for a second interview. Before any candidates are called back, the manager must finish the first round of interviews. This will take at least a week, so the candidate will hear nothing from the company and the company will hear nothing from the candidate for an extended period of time. This can be devastating. The candidate doesn't know whether the company is interested, and the hiring manager doesn't know if the candidate is interested. All sorts of things can happen during the intervening period of time.

The candidate may like the position, but this means very little in light of a firm offer from another company. Not knowing if the preferred company is at all interested, the candidate must go for the other company's offer. The hiring manager has the same problem, preferring one candidate but unsure of whether that candidate is interested in the position. By the time the candidate is notified that the company would like a second interview, the candidate has been forced to accept another position or lose out on a sure hire.

The best candidate may be gone, but the hiring process grinds on. One or two of the remaining candidates are brought back for a second interview two or three weeks after the first round is completed. Second interviews generally take longer and usually involve more people from the company. For this reason,

scheduling may take considerably longer. However, by the fifth week, assuming everything moves along at optimum speed, a decision is reached.

An offer is mailed to the candidate, giving him or her one week to respond. The company has no idea whether the candidate will accept the offer.

» Was the proposed salary acceptable?

If they were only $1000 short, they'll never know.

» Is the candidate considering three other offers?

The company doesn't know.

» Does the candidate have a concern or two that was never addressed?

The company hasn't a clue.

» Was the offer negotiable?

The candidate doesn't know.

Most candidates don't know how to negotiate an unacceptable offer. That's why only one in three offers made this way is accepted.

This means that there are two chances in three the company will have to go through the entire hiring process again. Six weeks have passed, and they are no closer to hiring someone than they were six weeks ago. However, they have wasted hundreds of hours without any results. At $50.00 an hour, this can get expensive.

A Better Way to Hire

Okay, so now it's your turn. How do you make this hiring mess better?

Let's go back to the original question.

When do you want this person actually reporting to work?

Let's say that it is now Friday, June 13. Between you and the manager, you decide that the person should report to work on Monday, July 15. That is just a little over four weeks away. From here you start working backward.

"Okay," you say to the hiring manager, "in order for a new employee to report to you on July 15, he or she must be able to notify their current employer that they are leaving their old position no later than July 1. It is only appropriate that they give their current employer two weeks notice that they have accepted a new position and that their last day in their current position will be Friday, July 12. That means you must have extended the offer of employment and it must have been accepted by Monday, July 1. This, of course, means that you must make your selection by Friday, June 28. Does that make sense?"

"Yes."

"Then, this means that the second interviews should be completed by Wednesday, June 26 so you'll have a day or two to review everything before the offer is extended. Do you agree?"

"Sounds right."

"Okay. That means that we will have to complete the entire first round of interviews by Friday, June 20. That's just a week from today. As I mentioned some time back, I will do all the preliminary screening and narrow the candidates down to a final four. You'll need to find time to interview these people by next Friday. Can I make a suggestion?"

"Certainly."

"Other hiring managers I have worked for find that things work best if an entire morning or afternoon is set aside for interviewing candidates. You get the whole thing over with at one time rather than dragging it out over days or weeks. This way you can focus on the hiring process without having continual interruptions. In fact, most managers like to do all the interviews in one afternoon away from the office. This way they can concentrate on the interviews without being interrupted except for emergencies. This has other advantages as well."

"Such as?"

"I'll be there to coordinate everything. I can introduce you to each candidate and keep you on schedule, if you like. When time is limited, a particularly talkative candidate can infringe on your time or the time you should be spending with another candidate. I can give you a signal so you'll know when you have about five minutes left with a particular candidate. This gives you the opportunity to wrap things up and close out the overly exuberant candidate who might otherwise upset your schedule.

"By meeting all the candidates at the same time under the same set of circumstances, you'll also eliminate the bias that occurs when interviews take place in a helter-skelter fashion. Under other circumstances, one candidate may get a lot of uninterrupted time, while a second candidate may get little actual time because of unforeseen interruptions and scheduling conflicts. The second candidate may be the better candidate, but you may not find this out if you are unable to spend quality time with that person. You could easily end up missing the best candidate.

"I can also debrief each candidate after the interview. As soon as all the candidates are interviewed, we'll be able to sit down together and compare information about each person. I'll be able to provide immediate information on how the candidates felt about the interview, the position and the company while the interviews are fresh in your mind.

"This will save you a lot of valuable time. Studies show that hiring managers can spend upward of forty hours getting through the first set of interviews. We can finish the entire process in five or six hours, at most. Does all this sound reasonable to you?"

"Certainly."

"If your schedule allows it, I suggest Friday afternoon, a time that's usually best for everyone, particularly since most of the candidates work and will have some difficulty getting away at other times. How does Friday afternoon look to you?"

"I have a meeting that runs until 2:30 that afternoon."

"That's okay. We can run the interviews from 3:00 to 7:00 in the evening. We can talk about them over dinner afterwards. My treat. Is there a place nearby where you like to eat?"

"I have a couple of ideas. We can decide

on that later."

"Okay, so the first interviews will take place on Friday, June 20th, from 3:00 to 7:00 P.M."

You now have agreement number five.

One other small chore remains to be accomplished.

You say, "It's never to early to start arranging for the second interviews. I recommend that two finalists come back for a second interview. That way, if something happens to your first choice, you always have a back up candidate. You mentioned that the finalists will be meeting three other people in your company, so we'll have to coordinate schedules. Since the second interviews must be completed by Wednesday, the 26th, it's not too early to set up the times for the second set. Between now and Friday, I will be screening candidates so we can get down to the best final four. Can you begin making the necessary arrangements with the people in your company so we can schedule the second interviews?"

"Sure."

"Great. I think we're all set then. I'll be there around 2:30 on Friday to make sure things run smoothly."

Final Agreements

15. Most positions are open either because a new position was just approved or because someone has vacated an existing position. New positions are easy to sell. A new position usually means that the company and the department are growing. This is attractive to ambitious candidates who want some assurance of future growth potential.

Vacated positions are another story. If the position was vacated because someone was promoted, that's good news. Like the new position, it shows that the company and the department are growing. However, if someone left the company, voluntarily or at the request of the company, this is generally viewed as bad news. In order to fill the position with the best possible people, you must know the complete story behind the vacated position. You must know why the previous employee left. Potential candidates need to know precisely what took place, so the best candidate will not hesitate to come on board. Most candidates will be willing to explore the opportunity once they have heard the real story.

16. Now is the time to let the manager know what it will cost for your exceptional services. In most cases, they will be aware that the services of recruiters cost money, but it is best to be sure. Generally, you should first ask, "Have you ever worked with recruiters before?"

If the answer is yes, follow-up with, "Our fees are basically identical to the fees of most agencies in the area. That is, we charge a fee equal to 30% of the annual salary offered to the candidate you hire. In other words, if you hire a candidate at $40,000, our fee will be 30% of $40,000, or $12,000."

If the manager has not previously worked with a recruiter, you must advise him or her that there is a fee involved for your service. Then explain what the fee will be.

Let the hiring manager know that you will be sending a letter to confirm your willingness to do the search. The letter will confirm the fee and the guarantee. For more on negotiating fees and guarantees, see Chapter Ten.

You now have your sixth agreement.

Now that you and the hiring manager have put together a hiring program that is practical and effective for both parties, it is time to look at the information needed to ensure that you can attract the very best candidates. Regardless of what others may believe, recruiters cannot get a candidate to change positions or to interview for another position if it is not in the candidate's best interest to do so. All a recruiter can do is make sure that the candidate has the best information available in order to make the *right* decision.

Generally, people confront just a few major decisions in their lifetimes. At the top are decisions about whom to marry and where to live. Career decisions usually rank number three on the list, higher for some people. For this reason, talking to people about changing jobs is not something to take lightly, especially if you want to provide your client with the best available candidates.

No candidate worth his beans is going to interview for a position just because you think he should. Before making such a commitment, a candidate will want a lot of information and will ask a lot of questions. With the help of the hiring manager, you must put together the information necessary to help the candidates make an informed decision. Items #17 through #27 are designed with this in mind.

17. Benefits have become a major issue. The average benefit package now amounts to one-fourth or one-third of an employee's annual salary.

People have different needs. Medical insurance may not mean much to a candidate covered by a spouse's medical plan, while it might be the most important factor to another candidate. A candidate may have a non-working spouse or one who must pay a large premium; whereas your client might pay the entire premium. In cases like this, your client's company might save the candidate as much as $4000 or $5000 a year with this benefit alone. So too might retirement plans the company offers, particularly if the retirement fund is contributed to in part by the company. Plans such as a 401k that shield employees' earnings from income tax deductions are of great value. Stock options, profit sharing plans and bonuses all have value if the company is doing well. Generally, the hiring manager can give you a history of how these benefits have paid off in the past.

Once you have the benefit information together, try to attach a reasonable money value to them. This can be an important factor in a candidate's decision to interview for the position. It could be a critical factor when the time comes to offer employment to one of your candidates on behalf of your client. The value of the benefits may determine whether the candidate accepts or declines the offer.

18. Why would a person be willing to accept the position? This is a question for the hiring manger, who will most likely expound on the nice, friendly people in their group, the great learning opportunity available, the wonderful company, and other warm and fuzzy issues. Don't forget to mention these to potential candidates. It may not seem important to you, but it may be just what a candidate wants to hear.

19. The reason why the hiring manager decided to work for this particular company and why he or she has stayed with the company will often provide a vital recruiting tool. You will be able to give potential candidates some insight into the hiring manager's personality and describe why that person would be great to work for. Managers often reach into their hearts to answer this question, so listen carefully.

20. Although you may never have worked in an accounting department or a data processing department, the potential candidates have. When you describe the size and structure of the department, the candidate will be able to determine a good deal about the position.

The structure of the department will also tell the candidate a good deal about the hiring manager's management style and whether there are strict or flexible lines of authority within the department. Each candidate will have a different preference. Some flourish in structured environments and some do better in unstructured environments. It's best to weed out incompatible candidates early in the game.

21. Positions that can lead to promotion or that offer a definite career path are always the most attractive. Unfortunately, this is something that is seldom thought out when a position opens up. Therefore, you will seldom receive a concrete answer. However, it doesn't hurt to ask, for promotion possibilities are dynamite selling points.

More frequently, the position will provide learning opportunities that prepares the candidate for the next step up the career ladder. This next step may take place within the company or may require moving on to another company. In any event, the position will help the candidate along the career path.

22. Almost every candidate wants to know what sort of business the client is in. Usually, this is just casual curiosity. However, sometimes it can be vital. Some candidates prefer working in certain industries while other candidates may want to avoid certain industries or products. For instance, certain people refuse to work for companies that are associated with the military or that are perceived as enemies of the environment. These same people may jump at the chance to work for a company that they perceive as anti-military or pro-environment.

23. Almost everyone is interested in the size of the company they work for. Many people want to avoid very large companies that they perceive as too bureaucratic. The two best barometers of this information are the company's annual sales and the number of employees in the company.

24. Most likely the company is going to have competitors. If the company is ranked among the top three in the marketplace, this can be a good selling point. The chances are that the company is stable and is going to be around for a long time. On the other hand, if the company is ranked number nineteen, this is probably a subject best forgotten. You might even think about whether the company will be around long enough to pay your fee.

25. If this location is not the company's headquarters, where is headquarters? How much control does HQ exert over the local office? How often might the employee being sought for this position be expected to go to the main office? Is this company a subsidiary of a larger corporation? If so, how much autonomy does it have? These are all bits of information that can make the position either more or less attractive to potential candidates.

26. Is the company's market local, regional, national or international? This is a question that has relevance to a position with considerable customer contact. People in sales and customer support positions are going to be particularly interested in the scope of the company's market. One candidate may envision the international marketplace as a means to international travel and high adventure. However, this same international marketplace may mean days away from home and family to another candidate.

27. While related to Item #24, which provides a ranking, this item paints an accurate picture of the company's real market share. A company may be ranked first and still have only a 10% share of the market if there are many competitors. On the other hand, a company that ranks third may have a 25% share of the market if there are few competitors. Items #24, #26 and #27 are of particular interest to candidates in sales and marketing. This information helps candidates visualize what the potential income might be if the position is based in part on commissions.

Items #28, #29 and #30 are designed to help you locate the candidate your hiring manager is sure to hire. They will also help you avoid sending candidates that the manager would never consider even though they have all the qualifications.

28. Most hiring managers would love to hire someone who already understands their business. A candidate with such knowledge requires much less training and, as a result, becomes an effective part of the team much more quickly. This is particularly true in sales but can be equally true for almost any discipline. The hiring manager will know the names of their competitors and, on occasion, will have some contacts within other companies. Hiring managers interested in hiring someone from the same industry will be happy to provide you with whatever information they may have.

This information can also be vital to your business as a recruiter. What could be more valuable than the names of other potential clients with hiring needs that fall within your area of specialization? For instance, if you are specializing in placing sales persons in the steel industry, every competitor the hiring manager names is a potential client. Similarly, every salesperson in these companies can become part of your ever-growing candidate database.

29. If the hiring manager would be happy to hire a candidate from Company X, any candidate you recruit from Company X is a virtual hire. Managers make these decisions when the other company operates in a fashion very similar to the hiring manager's company, or the other company has a very good reputation. This bias is going to carry over in the hiring

manager's ultimate decision.

30. This is the other side of Item #29. The hiring manager may have heard bad things about Company Y and doesn't want to hire anyone from such a disreputable company. Your assurance that you will not included any candidates from Company Y will increase the bond of confidence between you and the hiring manager. It will also strengthen the hiring manager's resolve to let you screen the candidates.

This doesn't mean you shouldn't recruit from Company Y to enlarge your database of candidates. After all, hiring managers from other companies may not carry the same bias. A search assignment is always a good tool for recruiting candidates. Just be careful not to submit any candidates from Company Y to this particular hiring manager.

Now that you are an expert in taking a good search assignment, let's discover where to find these search assignments.

CHAPTER 3

MARKETING CONCEPTS

IF PEOPLE LIKE YOU,
THEY'LL LISTEN TO YOU,
BUT IF THEY TRUST YOU,
THEY'LL DO BUSINESS
WITH YOU.

Finding a search assignment is an not nearly as hard as you might think, once you know where to look. There are dozens of places you can find search assignments, and as you become more experienced you will discover many additional sources. Meantime, let's look at several obvious sources of search assignments.

Newspaper Advertisements

In every daily newspaper across the country, you'll see column after column of want ads placed by companies looking to hire certain professionals. If you've picked a relatively popular profession to specialize in, there may be several pages of want ads placed by dozens of companies. Some recruiters use the newspaper to help them choose the area where they want to specialize. This approach should be used with caution, however. If your local newspaper runs six pages of want ads for software engineers every week, you will obviously have no trouble getting search assignments. However, you may have a great deal of trouble filling them because of the lack of candidates in your area.

While newspaper want ads provide a barometer of the demand for certain professionals, there are many exceptions. Most physicians and lawyers, for instance, while always in great demand are almost never solicited through want ads. Certain professions disdain using newspaper want ads.

There are several drawbacks to using the want ads as a source of search assignments, but they can be overcome with proper training. The first drawback is that every other recruiter and recruiting agency dealing with your professional group will be calling the company in an attempt to work on filling the position. This may seem like a great disadvantage; after all, who likes competition? However, in the next chapter you will learn how to turn this disadvantage into an advantage.

Another drawback is that the company is usually convinced it will get the right candidate through the want ads and therefore does not need the services of a recruiter. As you will learn in the next chapter, the company shouldn't make this decision. *You* should.

Despite these minor problems, want ads in newspapers are an excellent source of potential search assignments and each one should be explored. Where else are you going to find fifty to 100 notices each week from companies looking for the very professionals you specialize in? We'll talk about how to deal with companies who insist on using want ads later this chapter, but right now let's learn how to locate some of the 60% or 65% of the positions that are not advertised in the paper. That's right, only about 35% to 40% of all open positions are advertised in your daily newspaper. Where are the others hiding?

Your Database

Successful recruiters continually expand their database of candidates. The effective recruiter not only regards the database as a source of candidates for filling positions, but as a fount of valuable information. Every member of the database is working, and all are aware of what's happening in their workplace. They know when a new position is about to open up and when someone is about to vacate an existing position.

Talk to the people in your database. Make them your friends. They will tell you what is happening in their work environment, and you will be the first to know when a position is opening up. Things are always in a state of change. Today's happy employee could be disillusioned tomorrow and an eager candidate the day following. If you stay in contact with these events, you can have the replacement position filled long before other recruiters find out there ever was a vacancy. Candidates in my database frequently call me and tell me about a position they just heard about. Sometimes they will even ask me to represent them to the company.

Interviews

A good recruiter soon learns the value of a proper interview. When you interview candidates, you mine a valuable resource. Candidates will not only be aware of openings in their current or recently-vacated work environment but also where they have interviewed or applied.

Interviews are the key components in activities that link search assignments with candidates. The interview is so important that you'll find an entire chapter devoted to it. For now, however, remember these two things:

» The interview is a vital resource for finding out about position openings.

» Interview candidates in your exact area of specialization only.

If you forget either of these two important considerations, your effectiveness as a recruiter will diminish.

Reference Checks

Reference checks can serve as a great resource for finding search assignments. To take full advantage of the resources that reference checks offer, you must get the right references from a candidate. This is usually done during the interview process. Many candidates will have worked for more than one company and you will want the names of all the hiring managers the candidate has worked for. Later, you'll learn how to get the right information and how to turn these reference checks into search assignments.

Of course, the candidate from whom you obtain references must be a professional who works directly within your area of specialization. Otherwise, any information you get will be essentially worthless. Any position you might glean from a candidate outside your area of specialization will be difficult if not impossible to fill because it will call for professionals not found in your database. Attempting to fill positions outside your area of specialization will waste weeks of your time. Too many such attempts will put you out of business.

Telemarketing

Telemarketing has received a deservedly bad name. Poorly performed telemarketing can make an otherwise gentle person angry and abusive. However, when properly performed, telemarketing is one of the best ways to find search assignments. You can pick up a great many search assignments this way if you remember a few basic rules:

1. The person about to answer the phone is in the middle of something and may resent the interruption. Start the conversation by apologizing for the interruption. It's surprising how seldom this is done and how much it is appreciated. When you take the time to acknowledge that the person you're calling is busy, you're saying you know he or she is an important person. This is always appreciated.

2. Introduce yourself immediately and address the person you've called by his or her first name. This will set the tone for your relationship. Some recruiters find it difficult to address strangers, especially those in high position, by their first names. However, to set up the agreements discussed in the last chapter, you and the person on the other end of the phone must view each other as equals. The hiring manager—the president of the company, for that matter—must regard you as much a professional in your line of business as they are in theirs. This should be true of all the phone calls you make, not just telemarketing calls.

3. Always have something to offer. Since you are interrupting someone's day, make the interruption worth it. What you have to offer will depend upon your area of specialization, but it could involve something

as simple and straightforward as an assessment of the marketplace.

4. Don't make the first call a marketing call. On occasion, the first call will produce a search assignment, but this should not be your goal. Your goal should be to get acquainted with the person and to make arrangements for a call-back at a later date.

5. Follow-up all calls with a note or letter thanking people for taking the time from their busy schedule to talk with you. Take the opportunity to reconfirm the time you'll be calling them back. We'll go into this in more detail next chapter.

Some people find telemarketing a difficult or unpleasant task, but it is one of the best ways to make new acquaintances in your area of specialization and to get search assignments that no other recruiter will have. Nothing is more satisfying than a search assignment that is yours and yours alone. Think of telemarketing as a great way to develop new friends in your area of specialization, and you will start looking forward to it.

The Yellow Pages

If you are working with professionals in a specific industry, the *Yellow Pages* is a great source of information. Your local library will have the *Yellow Page* listings for your entire geographic area. You can also order telephone books from the phone company at no charge. Whether you are working in the medical field, the metals industry, or elsewhere, every company looking for the professionals you specialize in will be listed in the *Yellow Pages.* You can acquire an entire client list from this source. There are also industry-wide registers, journals and guides in most areas of specialization. *Lit-erary Market Place* (LMP), for example, is the bible of the publishing industry.

Professional Organizations

Joining professional organizations is another good way to meet the people you will be working with and for. Almost every profession has one or more professional organizations set up to exchange ideas, socialize, and present a united front when something threatens the profession. Recruiters are always welcome and often serve as officers on organization boards. The more frequently you attend meetings of these organizations, the more potential candidates and hiring managers you will meet. Hiring managers as well as candidates feel more comfortable dealing with a recruiter they've met in person, someone they feel they know and can trust.

Professional Publications

Professional trade publications are filled with pertinent information. Sometimes the author of an article will also be a hiring manager. It never hurts to call and congratulate that person for writing a fine article. Professional publications frequently have a special section where positions are advertised. You can pursue these just as you would want ads in the newspaper. Many of these publications can be found in the local library if you don't want to subscribe to them, while subscriptions to many trade publications are available at no cost.

Internal Spy

It might be worth while cultivating a friend at companies that employ many professionals in your area of specialization, someone who will keep an eye on things for you. Certain departments within a company have a lot of contact with the public, while other departments have virtually no contact with the public. Isolated employees love to hear from people outside the company and are easy to befriend. My favorite department for this purpose is building maintenance.

Your friend's task is easy. Every company has a bulletin board where details are posted on all the positions the company has open. Your friend's job is simply to check the bulletin board periodically and let you know when a position in your area of specialization is posted. You will know about this opening weeks before any other recruiter is aware of it.

Industry Specific Network

Some professions are particularly industry-specific. Recruiters who deal with sales professionals, for example, will almost always deal with salespeople in only one or two selected industries. It's obviously impossible to maintain a database of sales professionals for every industry in the world. Recruiters who deal with medical professionals are sometimes industry specific as well. For instance, some may deal only with hospitals while others may deal only with group medical practices.

In any event, if your recruiting efforts are industry specific, there may be several industry networks to tap into. By joining one of these networks, you become privy to the industry's scuttlebutt. This gossip often includes information about who is looking for an employee and who is about to leave a position. This network can place you light years ahead of the competition in getting the search assignment.

Incoming Calls

As you become more established in your area of specialization, you will begin to get calls from old clients who enjoyed working with you in the past. They will call with new positions they want you to fill. Sometimes it will be a position outside your area of specialization, and this is the time to call in your friendly fellow-recruiter. Don't try to build a database of candidates you will need to fill this one position; share the assignment with a recruiter who specializes in this other profession. Getting 50% of a $10,000 fee is not bad, especially when you have to do very little of the work.

Now that you know where you can look for search assignments, it's time to learn about who *you* are and about who the people you contact *think* you are.

WHO YOU ARE AND WHAT YOU DO

Everyone has a different perception about what a recruiter does. If you are going to be a successful recruiter, you need to understand exactly who you are and what you do.

Not every recruiter is the same, not by a long shot. Recruiters not only work different markets (professions), different recruiters work different ways. Some recruiters deal primarily with big companies and truckloads of resumés. They're not much different than the recruitment agencies described earlier. Other recruiters view themselves as specialists in the fields where they've chosen to recruit, and they think that clients should love them because they're so knowledgeable about the profession in which they've chosen to recruit.

However, truly successful recruiters soon realize that their real expertise is in the hiring process. Once recruiters really understand this concept, they are no longer merely the people that clients contract with to fill a position they are unable to fill themselves. Instead, they become the experts clients turn to for assistance with any number of issues that arise in the personnel arena.

Since most recruiters function like agencies, most clients view them as just another source of resumés. Therefore, it is best to assume that a potential new client will see you as just another agency or a recruiter who works like an agency. You'll have to demonstrate that you're a different breed, a *real* recruiter.

Consultant

You will soon have a firm grasp of what salaries are being offered to professionals within your specialty. If you let potential clients know you have this information, you will start getting calls. I get a lot of calls around budget time from hiring managers who plan to hire people next fiscal year and need to budget a salary for the positions. Who better to ask about salaries than a recruiter who always has a finger on the pulse of the hiring process for that profession? It's great to help a client put together a more accurate budget while, at the same time, learning that there will soon be a new opening for you to fill.

As time goes by, you will discover other things that will benefit your potential clients. This information can help break the ice or provide the *raison d'être* when making marketing calls.

Resource

Smart recruiters make potential clients aware that they should be seen as resources and tapped whenever the need arises. Because you specialize in a particular profession, your primary job is to stay in constant contact with people working in the profession. Therefore, you frequently hear about new ideas and processes, or new approaches to old problems. Clients should be encouraged to call you, which is not to say that you are going to have the answer in your hip pocket but that you can find the answer or put them in contact with someone who has the answer. This is a wonderful excuse for contacting another potential client or two and for calling this client back. When the time comes to fill a position, they will know whom to call.

Time Saver

Not only have hiring managers little experience in hiring people, most of them hate the hiring process. Most see it as a long, time-consuming, thankless chore. Your job is to convince them that it can be a simple process that won't take much time at all. Looking at it from their perspective, using the old hiring process, they can spend between eighty and 100 hours trying to hire someone. Using your methods, you can save the hiring manager a lot of time, and time is money. By cutting the amount of time spent on the hiring process from 100 hours to eight hours, you will have saved the hiring manager ninety-two hours, that's ninety-two hours that can be spent doing the things the hiring manager was trained and hired to do.

There are only two reasons why hiring managers might object to such a plan:

» They were trained by previous recruiters to expect nothing more from you than a bunch of resumés with the right buzz words;

» They don't feel confident that you can properly screen candidates and come up with the best final four. What you learned last chapter should come to your rescue. After all, being able to come up with the right candidates depends on nothing more than good communications between you and the manager.

Guarantor

You are going to *guarantee* that the manager will be able to hire the desired candidate. It doesn't hurt to point out that this is a rather remarkable guarantee, especially since two out of every three offers of employment are normally turned down. You can make such a guarantee, however, because you have been intimately involved in the hiring process from the moment you discussed the search assignment with the manager, and you will continue to be involved until the chosen candidate is sitting at his or her new desk in the client's company. As the hiring process proceeds, you will make sure that the candidates concerns are all addressed, that all expectations are met, that the proper offer is extended and that the candidate does not accept a counter offer. All this will be covered in detail in Chapter 9.

Confidential Source

The hiring process is not always intended to be a public matter. There are frequently times when it is important that certain hiring take place without others being aware of it. If you scrutinize the want ads you will notice there are many ads that do not list the name or otherwise reveal the identity of the company that placed the ad. Referred to in the industry as "blind ads," they may be run because a company does not want a competitor to know it is in the process of hiring professionals in certain areas. Blind ads are also run when a company is planning to replace an employee but doesn't want the employee to know he or she is about to be replaced.

Trying to maintain confidentiality with want ads is difficult. In the first place, it isn't always very hard to figure out what company is running the ad. There's also a good chance that the person, or a friend of the person about to be replaced, will see some of the resumés that are sent in response to the ad and start to ask questions. Imagine how the sole controller in a company is going to feel if a friend asks, "How come our company is running ads for a new controller?" Then there are the interviews. How is the hiring manager or personnel director going to conduct interviews without others knowing that something is going on?

It's easy to see how a recruiter could be very effective in a hiring situation where confidentiality is important. Should the recruiter need to run an ad (which really shouldn't be necessary to begin with), there is no way it can be traced back to the client's company. No one in the client's company will see any resumés because none will be sent to the company. Finally, all the interviews can take place away from the client's company where they will never be observed by anyone connected with the company.

Impartial Screener

Companies often face another dilemma where recruiters can be a big help. When promotion time rolls around, things can get very uncomfortable inside a company. When a supervisory or management position opens up, several employees within the company may well be eligible, or at least think they are eligible, for that promotion. Most companies would like to get the best possible candidate for the position, and this means looking at candidates outside as well as inside the company. No matter whom the company eventually selects, there are going to be some hurt feelings, and the company is going to look like the bad guy. Employees who have been passed over may think about leaving.

All this can be avoided by using a recruiter. The recruiter can screen candidates within and outside the company and make recommendations about who should be hired. The company need not take the recruiter's advice, but it does take the heat off the company. The internal candidates will know that all the candidates were screened by an impartial resource outside the company. Anger will be directed away from the company. When appropriate, remind a potential client that this service is available. The fee will generally be different than the fee for a successful search. Most recruiters charge by the hour. However, if the client also wants you to do a search for possible candidates, a standard fee is in order.

Data Base Maintainer

Whenever a company needs to hire a particular professional, it must start the search from scratch. Companies rarely maintain a database of candidates to draw from. Even if they have hired a particular professional in the past and have a few resumés sitting around, the resumés will be old and virtually worthless. Even if the company can locate the individuals who once sent in resumés, those they locate will most likely have found other employment. A recruiter, on the other hand, is in constant contact with people in his or her database and is constantly adding to it. Therefore, the recruiter will have an active, viable database from which the company can draw. Most companies completely overlook this function, although it is routinely performed by recruiters.

Promoter of the Profession

If you want special recognition from hiring managers in the profession you have chosen to specialize in, promote the profession. This takes imagination and varies from profession to profession, but I will share one activity that placed me at the head of the class among my competitors.

There was once an extreme shortage of people being trained to work in the technical area in which I specialize, a situation that greatly concerned me and the managers I work with. Managers were stealing candidates from one another (admittedly, sometimes with my help), and salaries were getting out of hand. It was uncomfortable for everybody, and finally I got some managers to discuss the situation. I contacted 150 managers, and about thirty became active in designing a program to train new people to work in the profession. We approached a local college and impressed the dean with the amount of support we were able to generate. Using the program designed by the managers, relevant courses were added to the college curriculum. I became the liaison between the college and the hiring managers, and now I automatically get twenty to thirty new candidates each year for my database when students complete the course. Every spring, just before graduation, I sponsor a career day where all the companies are invited to meet the new graduates. Everyone in the profession identifies this training program with me and credits me with solving a big personnel problem. It takes very little of my time, but gives me something to talk about every time I make a call.

Now that you know who you are, let the rest of the world know. Remember, most of your potential clients will think of you as just another recruitment agency *unless you take the time to advise them otherwise.*

HOW DO COMPANIES HIRE?

Companies use many different methods for recruiting and hiring professionals. It's important to understand the methods a company might use and why it uses a particular method. For instance, you know that a popular method for finding employees is through want ads. However, want ads are unproductive in finding certain professionals. Many companies use recruiters to fill positions, even those that say they don't, but how and when they use recruiters differs from company to company.

Why is it important to discuss other hiring methods? Because they are as much a part of your competition as are other recruiters.

As a general rule, companies will try to make the recruiting and hiring process as inexpensive as possible. They perceive that certain methods of hiring employees are less expensive

than other methods. Unfortunately, the only costs the average company calculates when making this determination are the direct costs of recruiting. They seldom consider the indirect costs of hiring and, as a result, these indirect costs are rarely identified. Listed in the order that companies generally perceive them as costing, from the least expensive to the most expensive, here are the chief methods they use to fill vacancies.

In-house Referrals

The human resources department of most companies believe that the least expensive way to hire a new employee is through a referral from another employee within the company. Basically, the process amounts to sending all the employees in the company a notice announcing that the company is looking for a particular professional. It's hoped that one or more employees will know a suitable professional and will talk this professional into joining the company. The direct costs of this method are practically nil. However, the chances of this method working are slight. Most employees will not be in contact with anyone from this particular profession. Many employees don't want to take responsibility for making recommendations for fear they may be blamed if things don't turn out well.

While referrals may be the least expensive way of hiring someone, it can become expensive if it is allowed to continue for very long. There are many indirect costs that accumulate as time goes by and the position remains unfilled. In sales, these costs are rather obvious. A sales position generates revenue for the company directly, and if it sits vacant the company is going to lose money. When you think about it, almost every position directly or indirectly impacts a company's revenue producing capacity. Any position left vacant for very long is going to have a negative impact on the company's income. And so, while an in-house referral system can be a good, money saving method of finding employees, it should not be used to the exclusion of methods that have a better chance of being productive.

In-house referrals do not address another high cost problem previously touched upon: namely, the high cost of hiring. Someone is going to have to review every referral. Employees who refer candidates will also expect some recognition for their efforts. Without feedback, they will never refer anyone again. Therefore, if the company expects the internal referral system to work, someone must acknowledge each referral. Providing this type of individualized feedback can be very time consuming.

Since employees who make the referrals are not experts in the hiring process, efforts spent arranging and conducting interviews can also be time consuming. Finally, after spending time acknowledging the referrals and conducting interviews, there is no guarantee that the desired candidate will be hired. Only a recruiter using the methods described in Chapter 9 can make such a guarantee. When you examine the indirect costs involved in a poorly managed in-house referral program, a recruiter's fee seems small by comparison.

Employee Bonus Program

When companies find that the employee referral program is not producing any candidates, someone in the human resources department is going suggest sweetening the pot. The idea is to offer a bounty or bonus to the in-house

employee who refers a candidate that the company hires. After all, paying your own employee $1,000 is a whole lot cheaper than paying a recruiter $10,000. Hundreds of employees will now start looking under every stone for the right candidate to claim that thousand dollar bonus.

Unfortunately, the same indirect costs we found in the original referral program are still present. The position may be filled a little more quickly, it's true, and this will save some of the costs incurred by keeping a position vacant for a period of time; however, these savings may be more than offset by the expense of hundreds of employees recruiting for the company on company time. Imagine what it costs a company if 150 employees spend fifteen hours of company time recruiting for a particular professional instead of doing the job they were hired to do. If the average employee earns $20 per hour in salary and benefits, this recruiting effort would cost the company $45,000. It makes a professional recruiter's fee look small by comparison, doesn't it?

Remember, no one in the company is going to be aware of these indirect costs unless you make them aware of it.

Want Ads

Want ads are an institution in America. Companies have been using them to advise the public of their hiring needs for many years, and yet no one has evaluated them to determine if they are an effective method for hiring *professionals*. However, a few things are obvious.

First, want ads are expensive. An individual ad may cost as little as $200 for a small ad to as much as four or five thousand dollars for a large display ad. And that's just for one weekend. (Most employees who are seeking a position, look at the want ads in the Sunday paper, so that's when most of the ads are run.) Seldom does a company find the right candidate the first time an ad is run, particularly if a good professional is being sought. Companies sometimes test the waters by placing an ad before calling a recruiter, which accounts for many ads that run only once or twice. On the other hand, I have seen ads run every week for twenty straight weeks. Frequently, a company will spend more money on want ads than they would have spent hiring a recruiter.

The costs might be tolerable if there were some guarantee that hiring would result, but there isn't. In fact, it is in the newspaper's best interest that the company doesn't hire someone. As long as a company is unable to find a good candidate, it will continue to run the ad and the newspaper will continue to make money. Recruiters, by comparison, have a vested interest in making sure that the company hires someone. Otherwise, the recruiter has worked for nothing. This is a very important issue. Whether the company chooses to use want ads or a recruiter, it is going to cost the company money. The difference is in the guarantee. The newspaper demands that the company pay money up front but makes absolutely no guarantee that the company will find someone to hire. The recruiter guarantees that the company will not spend a single penny unless the company hires someone. The recruiter can in all honesty say, "We guarantee that you will make a hire or it won't cost you a penny." No newspaper would even consider making such a guarantee.

Want ads offer the same limited service as

the referral and bonus systems: a peripatetic search for a candidate. They do absolute nothing to help defray the indirect costs of the traditional hiring process. Can you imagine the costs accumulated by a company that allows a position to sit vacant while a want ad runs for twenty weeks? And after finding a candidate, the company still faces a long hiring process, one that might need to be repeated two or three times. It doesn't hurt to remind your clients again and again that the recruiter offers a hiring program that saves the company and its employees time while making sure that the company hires the candidate it really wants.

The want ad system has another significant drawback. Only people specifically looking at the want ads are going to know that a position is available. Unless they are unemployed or unhappy with their current employment, they are not going to be reading the want ads in the weekend paper. Normally, between 2% and 5% of the professionals in a given field will be looking for a new position, so only a small percentage of the people a company wants to reach are going to know about the position. Under the circumstances, the chances of getting the best candidate are rather poor. A good recruiter, one who has taken the time to build a proper database of candidates, can make 90% to 95% of the people in a profession aware of the position. The chances of the company getting just the right candidate are considerably enhanced by using a recruiter.

There is another problem with hiring candidates through want ads. The people answering these ads are, for the most part, unemployed. An unemployed candidate is going to have a completely different motive for accepting a position than an employed candidate who is recruited. When people are out of work and the weekly paychecks are no longer coming in, their motives for accepting a position can be clouded by the need for income. They are much more likely to accept positions they don't really like when cash is running low. Unfortunately, these candidates are not likely to stay in their new positions very long. They will continue to watch the want ads or contact their recruiter for something better. When they leave, the company must start the search all over again.

Recruited candidates have totally different motives for accepting a position. Since they are currently employed, the pay-check motive will not exist. Recruited candidates move to new companies and new positions because the new situation offers them something special that their old position lacked. Money spent on recruited candidates is money well spent. They will stay with the new company for a long time.

HOW COMPANIES BENEFIT BY USING RECRUITERS

Companies that believe that engaging a recruiter is the most expensive way to hire a professional are looking only at direct costs and not hidden (indirect costs). When all costs are considered, the recruiter often offers the least expensive means of hiring professionals. Using a recruiter is the only way that a company can guarantee it will not spend a penny on the recruiting and hiring process unless a chosen candidate is actually hired. This has got to be worth something to most companies. Finally, hiring a recruited candidate considerably lessens the probability that the new employee will leave shortly after joining the company. The company, therefore, needs to go through the hiring process only once. When all these things are considered, using a recruiter becomes the least expensive way to hire a professional.

Inertia has kept an outworn hiring system in place in this country, and few recruiters have done anything to correct the misconception because most employ the same inefficient methods. Most people who work in personnel agencies and human resources departments within companies are unaware these problems even exist. This makes your job somewhat tougher and provides you with a unique and financially rewarding opportunity.

Read this chapter over and over until you understand everything it contains. You must completely understand the marketing concepts associated with hiring and the real benefits to client companies that engage a professional recruiter before you are ready to make your first marketing call.

CHAPTER 4

MAKING THE MARKETING CALL

YOU NEVER KNOW TILL
YOU TRY TO REACH THEM
HOW ACCESSIBLE PEOPLE
ARE; BUT YOU MUST
APPROACH EACH PERSON
BY THE RIGHT DOOR.

— HENRY WARD BEECHER

Before making a marketing call, you must first determine who is most likely to be the hiring manager of the professionals you've decided to represent. For instance, if you specialize in accounting professionals, you'll probably want to talk to a company's comptroller or accounting manager; if you specialize in computer professionals, you'll probably want to talk to the information systems manager or M.I.S. manager; if you specialize in sales professionals within an industry, you'll probably want to talk to the sales manager, etc.

The next step is to develop a *marketing list*. To do this, you'll need the Marketing Worksheet on pages 51–52 and either the *Yellow Pages* of the telephone books in your service area, a business directory, or some other reference source that lists the businesses in your service area. If you are specializing in a particular industry, such as pharmaceuticals, banking, or metals, you'll find many books in your library that list all the companies whose products fall into your particular area of specialization.

Ask the reference librarian for assistance.

When you are ready to assemble your first marketing list, open your reference book. You can start anywhere—beginning, middle or end—it doesn't make much difference. Your job is to search for companies that employ the professionals you specialize in. If your area is industry specific, every company in the book you checked out of the library is a target company. However, if you are specializing in placing accountants, computer programmers, or other professionals that almost every company hires, your approach will be different. When using the *Yellow Pages,* you can move from section to section. Companies that appear to be into manufacturing, distributing, wholesaling or warehousing products are almost sure to need professionals in your area of specialization. The headquarters of any business is going to need your professionals. In fact, any business with fifty or more employees or with annual sales of $5 million or more is likely to need the people you specialize in. Basically, the only thing to avoid are retail stores, cleaners, mortuaries, and businesses that are very small or are retail outlets for a company whose headquarters is elsewhere.

Write the name and telephone number of each potential client company on the Marketing Worksheet. Work from a list of at least fifty new companies every day. There are twenty-five spaces on each side of the Marketing Worksheet. Once you have fifty companies with their phone numbers listed, you are ready for the next step.

After you have been in the business for a month or two, you'll begin to get search assignment leads from some of the other resources listed in Chapter 3. If your resource is a newspaper want ad or if you got the information during an interview, you can anticipate that there is a position open at that company. However, you should not let this information influence how you conduct your day.

GETTING A NAME

In filling out the Marketing Worksheet, your first task will be to learn the name of the hiring manager. You do this by calling the company. If you're real lucky, you can determine his or her name just by asking the person who answers the phone. "Would you give me the name of your comptroller (or sales manager, etc.), please?" In most cases, however, the person answering the phone will want to know why you need the name. I generally say that I represent some professional organization. For example, I might say, "I'm with The Association of Accounting Professionals, and I need to mail some information to the comptroller. What is his full name?" If this doesn't get you the name, thank the operator and hang up. There are other ways to reach your goal.

In every company, there are people who frequently interact with the public and those who virtually never have contact with the public. People who frequently interact with the public— operators, receptionists, secretaries, human resource people, for instance—are trained not to give out employees' names, and they are particularly cautious about revealing a manager's name. Even by claiming that you just want to mail them something, you'd be lucky to get half the names of the managers you want from the people answering company phones. Some of them really take their training

50

MARKETING WORKSHEET

No	COMPANY	NAME	PHONE	COMMENTS	ACTION
1					
2					
3					
4					
5					
6					
7					
8					
9					
10					
11					
12					
13					
14					
15					
16					
17					
18					
19					
20					
21					
22					
23					
24					
25					

MARKETING WORKSHEET

	COMPANY	NAME	PHONE	COMMENTS	ACTION
26					
27					
28					
29					
30					
31					
32					
33					
34					
35					
36					
37					
38					
39					
40					
41					
42					
43					
44					
45					
46					
47					
48					
49					
50					

to heart, and that's when you should talk to someone who hasn't been trained to answer phones.

You can generally find these people in maintenance, the mail room, the clerical pool, data processing, and other areas where employees deal strictly with internal company matters. My favorite is the mail room because they know everybody, so that's where you might want to place your next call. The conversation might go something like this:

Clerk: Mail room.

You: Who?

Clerk: This is the mail room.

You: You must be kidding. Boy, did that operator send me to the wrong place. I'm sorry I disturbed you. I was trying to get the comptroller.

Clerk: No problem. I'll transfer you.

You: You know, I think the operator could use a little help. I think I'd have a better chance of getting where I was supposed to go if I could ask for the person by name. Do you happen to know the name of the comptroller? I'd hate to end up back here bothering you again.

Clerk: Sure. Just ask for Robin Jones.

You: Thanks for your help. Sorry to have disturbed you.

Now that you have Robin's name, enter it on your Marketing Worksheet.

Continue in this manner until you have listed the names of all the people you want to talk with on your worksheet. Once you've completed this task, you'll have your marketing list for the day. The first thing you'll do each day will be to make a marketing list for that day.

NOTE: Once you are well established, a good portion of your list will be made up of clients or people you have had previous contact with. However, even after many years in the business, some of the companies on your daily marketing list should be new. Continue to make new contacts because some of your client companies will be bought out or sold, go bankrupt, or be otherwise eliminated as clients. Always add new companies to your client base.

The Person on the Other End of the Line

Before you begin speaking with the potential hiring manager on your list, think about who will be on the other end of the line. When I call, I make several assumptions:

1. I assume that the potential hiring manager I've selected to call is very busy. Hiring managers not only must tend to their own responsibilities but must oversee and often deal with the responsibilities of their employees. This leaves little time for chit chat. Therefore, I want my call to be quick, to the point and demonstrate that it will save the hiring manager some time. However, above all, I want that person to understand that I know how busy he or she is, and I wouldn't have called if I didn't sincerely believe that it was in our mutual interests.

2. I assume that the potential hiring manager has spoken to other recruiters or recruiting agencies in the past. Most hiring managers, if they have been in their positions for any length of time, have been contacted by one or more recruiting agencies looking for business. The phrase, "looking for busi-

53

ness," is key. Most recruiters look for instant gratification in the form of search assignments. If one is not forthcoming, they move on without offering anything of substance. You want to make the hiring manager immediately aware that, regardless of who in the recruiting profession he or she has talked with in the past, you are different. In your own subtle way, you want that manager to know that you are calling to help. If this results in future business, that's fine, but it is not the purpose of this call. (If you are uncertain, review the section in Chapter 3 that discusses who you are.) You are calling to let the hiring manager know that there is a resource just a phone call away that can be called upon at any time.

3. I assume that the hiring manager is going to have a position available at some time in the future, and I want to be thought of when that occurs. However, I'm smart enough to know that few managers will think to call me when hiring time comes. It is going to be up to me to make the contact if I am going to get an opportunity to work on the search. Therefore, I will need to call this manager back at some time during the year. For this reason, my first call will include a brief discussion of the manager's hiring plans for the year. From the manager's point of view, any hiring plan is going to involve only those new positions budgeted for the year. However, there will most likely also be one or two unanticipated vacancies during the course of the year. Managers never plan for vacancies of this type, so it's your job to do so.

BEFORE MAKING THE CALL

As we discussed in Chapter 3, search assignments can be found by looking at want ads, joining professional organizations, and so forth. If a company advertises in the want ad section for an accountant, you can assume that it intends to hire an accountant, but your daily call list will not normally include many companies where you know, prior to calling, that a vacancy exists. Treat every call the same, regardless of whether you know or suspect that the hiring manager you are about to talk with has an opening. Don't let this knowledge influence your call.

Remember, you need only one placement each month to meet your financial goals. The best way to get that placement is to develop relationships that will lead to exclusive search assignments. Two or three exclusive search assignments will produce more placements than one hundred search assignments where you must compete with all the other recruitment entities in town to see who can send the best resumé to the human resources department.

Therefore, before making any call you should have several realistic goals in mind. It is unrealistic, for instance, to expect every phone call to uncover a search assignment, but it is not unrealistic to expect that a phone call can be the first step in a relationship that will eventually produce a search assignment. Some of your calls *are* going to produce an immediate search assignment, but do not make that your goal. The calls you are about to make are an investment in your future. With these thoughts in mind, let's look at some reasonable goals for your first phone call.

1. Your primary goal is to make this call the first step in building a relationship with the hiring manager, so that over time you will not be viewed as just another pesky recruiter. You would like to be viewed as a resource that the manager can call upon to help with any aspect of the hiring process.

2. A second goal is to inform the manager that your principal function is to save him or her time and the company money. When the time is right, you will eliminate all the hidden costs that make hiring such an expensive proposition for most companies.

3. Your third goal is to begin gathering information about the company, and especially the area of the company for which this manager is responsible. You will want to build a profile of the company so you can discuss its functioning intelligently with potential candidates. On page 65 is a form you can use as a guide in gathering the appropriate information. Don't expect to get all this information on the first call. It takes time.

4. Make sure you have something you can send to the manager through the mail. You want the manager to see your name in print. Sending something through the mail, along with your business card and a cover letter, will help the manager remember your name. What you send the manager may vary from company to company and from profession to profession. However, if you read the daily paper or a professional journal, you can always find something of interest to send. It's all right to send the same article to every manager you contact who has not already read it. Make sure you let the managers know you are sending the article, so they'll expect it and perhaps even look forward to it. Don't let more than a day or two elapse after calling to get something in the mail.

5. Your final goal is to arrange for a follow-up call. Let the manager know that you will be calling back at a certain time and for a certain reason, perhaps for nothing more than to ascertain that the material you sent was received. Alternately, the follow-up call may be for something as significant as providing information that will help fill a position. Just be sure to let the manager know that you will be calling back in a week, a month, two days—whatever—and why you will be calling. This is important. If managers know you are going to call them back in a week to make sure the U.S. Postal Service didn't lose the article you sent, they will treat the article with respect. They will watch for the article and place it within easy reach, so they will know where it is when you call back. Otherwise, the article (along with your card and letter) will end up in the back of a file or in the wastebasket. Make sure to record the time and date that you will make that follow-up call.

HANDLING THE MANAGER'S OBJECTIONS

No call should be considered a complete success unless you discover some of the objections a manager might have in working with you. The manager is sure to have many preconceived ideas about who you are and what you do. Unless you disabuse the manager of these preconceived notions, you will never have the kind of relationship that leads to exclusivity.

You must first uncover the preconceptions (objections) in order for the manager to understand who you really are and what you really do.

If you don't get any objections from the manager, you are probably doing something wrong—most likely not asking the right questions or asking dead-end questions. Questions that can be answered yes or no are examples of dead-end questions, because they preclude any further discussion. Answers to dead-end questions are sometimes referred to as closing answers.

> *Wrong Question:* "Have you had problems *in working with recruiters in the past?*"

> *Right Question:* "From what you've said, I suspect you have had some problems with recruiters in the past. What have been some of the biggest problems you have had to deal with?"

Ask the right question, and you will learn the manager's reservations about using recruiters. Then make sure you are perceived as different from other recruiters.

In many instances, an objection is an attempt at a quick brush-off. The manager doesn't want to deal with a recruiter at the moment. Therefore, in dealing with various objections, let's look at the objection first, then the underlying message, and then an appropriate response. As we cover the objections, remember everything you learned in the last chapter. All the answers are there.

Objection: "We don't use recruiters."

Interpretation: This is a quick brush-off. The manager doesn't want to deal with a recruiter, perhaps because there will be a hassle with personnel over paying a fee. All companies use recruiters at some time or another. There are certain positions that can't be filled any other way. What they are probably objecting to is paying a fee. If you offered to fill the position without charge the manager would have no objection at all.

Response: "I can understand that your company would not want to pay a fee unless it was absolutely necessary. How do you think they would react if I could save them money rather than cost them money the next time you need to fill a position?"

Objection: "We are currently (or will be) running an ad in the newspaper."

Interpretation: The manager is really saying, "We would rather hire people by running an ad in the newspaper than by using a recruiter. Recruiters are too expensive. This is the way we have always done it and it's safe. Nobody objects to the amount of money we spend on ads."

Response: "I can understand why you might think that a newspaper ad would be less expensive than using a recruiter. However, I will guarantee you that I won't cost you a single penny unless you actually hire a well-qualified candidate through my efforts. How do you think the newspaper would react if you asked them to make the same guarantee?"

It is important to understand and communicate one very basic concept. You are not asking to be paid a fee at this time, or at *any* time if you do not find a candidate that the company hires. If you decide to do some recruiting on the company's behalf, you will be doing it without charge. The hiring manager should have no objection to your working for nothing.

The decision to pay a fee need only be decided after the manager has seen what the newspaper has uncovered in the way of candidates and what you have uncovered in the way of candidates. If your candidates are superior, the manager may agree to pay you a fee for your work by hiring the candidate you uncovered. If you can't come up with a good enough candidate, the manager can hire the best one found through the newspaper ad. Its a win-win situation for the manager. No one is under any obligation to pay you anything unless one of your candidates is hired. Wouldn't it be nice if the newspaper had the same policy?

Objection: "You will be contacting the same candidates I can get through the newspaper."

Interpretation: The manager is honestly afraid that you will contact candidates that would have responded to the newspaper ad. The bottom line is financial once again. The cost of a newspaper ad is less than a recruiter's fee.

Response: "I can understand your concern. You certainly don't want to pay me for a candidate you could have gotten through your ad. However, what I am offering you is access to the 95% of the candidates not reading the want ads. They are people who are currently employed and have no reason to read the ads. I just want to make sure you get the very best candidate, regardless of whether it comes from me or from the ad."

Objection: "Recruiters cost too much money."

Interpretation: Here, the manager is only looking at direct costs and comparing it to the $10,000 fee that it's believed a recruiter will cost. The door is wide open on this one: almost everything in Chapter 3 addresses this is-

sue. If you are a bit of a gambler, you might offer the following challenge:

Response: "If you are willing to sit down with me and honestly evaluate all the costs incurred in hiring someone, I will guarantee that hiring through me will cost you less than hiring through a newspaper want ad. Why don't we meet tomorrow afternoon? That will give us both time to get all our facts and figures together."

Objection: "I'm already getting too many calls from recruiters. I don't have that kind of time."

Interpretation: This is a case where the manager has heard from a number of recruiters, perhaps because an ad has recently appeared in the newspaper. In reality, this is a brush-off. The manager is busy, doesn't want to deal with the problem at the moment, wants you to go away and not be a bother.

Response: "I'm sorry I picked a bad time to call, but maybe I can be of help. If you would like, I will teach the person who answers your phone how to screen calls to make sure you don't hear from other recruiters. Then you and I can get together to discuss your needs when you have more time. I can drop by tomorrow afternoon at 2:00 o'clock if that would be convenient."

Objection: "The last time I used a recruiter I was sent the wrong people. It was a big waste of time."

Interpretation: You have to sympathize with anyone who has had this experience. It's like being offered a glass of milk right after taking an inadvertent gulp of sour milk. While this could be a brush-off, it could well be true. A lot of agencies with untrained people could have sent this manager unqualified candidates. Here's a golden opportunity to help a manager who was willing to try an agency and got stung. In handling this objection, be careful not to sound like you are putting the other agency down.

Response: "I'm sorry you had such a bad experience. Often the problem is little more than a lack of good communication. If the recruiter you work with is willing to take the time to really listen to what you need, such a thing should never happen. It also helps to be sure that the recruiter you are working with specializes in working with the type of professionals you hire. How do you go about screening your recruiters to ensure you're working with the right one?"

Objection: "I already work with three agencies that I am very satisfied with. I don't need any more."

Interpretation: This may not be true, but you must assume it is. Like all other objections there is always the possibility that it is just a brush-off.

Response: "I'm glad to find someone who has taken the time to look for agencies that will do a good job. I can tell that you only want to work with the very best, and I too would like you to have the very best. Therefore, I'd like to make a deal with you. The next time you have an opening, give me a shot at it. If I don't do a better job than one or all the agencies you currently work with, I'll never bother you again. On the other hand, if I do a better job than they do, let me replace the one that does the worst job. I'd like to make this a win-win situation for you. When do you anticipate that

you'll have another opening that will need to be filled?"

Objection: "You'll have to talk to personnel. They handle everything having to do with hiring."

Interpretation: This is a tough one. It most likely is a brush-off. However, it is also quite possibly true. The hiring manager may have given control to human resources intentionally, or the personnel department may have the same control that is often found in the larger, bureaucratic companies. It is also possible that the company has specific policies for working with agencies and the manager wants you to discuss them with human resources before you proceed any further. In any event, you are eventually going to have to talk with personnel.

Response: "I'd be happy to talk with personnel. However, before I do, I want to make sure I do the very best possible job for you. Tell me exactly who it is that you would like to hire. No matter how hard we all try, something is lost when it is interpreted through a third party." At this point, you may want to pull out the your Search Assignment form from Chapter 2. "Can you tell me what you anticipate the day to day duties of this position to be?" Get as much information as possible before speaking with human resources.

While I cannot address every possible objection you will encounter, most will be variations of the ones above. With what you've already learned, you should be able to handle just about anything that might come your way.

HANDLING OBJECTIONS FROM HUMAN RESOURCES

Some recruiters find working through human resources so frustrating, they refuse to work with any company where human resources is involved in the hiring process. If you decide to work with human resources, you must expect certain things:

» You will have to go through several more steps in the hiring process.

» The process will take much longer.

» You may have to deal with resumés.

As long as you're willing to deal with these things, working with human resources offers certain rewards.

It isn't difficult to determine a hiring manager's priorities. Every manager wants to get the very best candidate on board as quickly as possible. However, dealing with human resources means working with an entirely different mindset and an entirely different set of priorities. Most people in human resources will tell you that their primary responsibility is not getting people hired. Many will even confess that they hate this part of their job. They see their priorities and functions this way:

1. Protecting the company from possible lawsuits involving improper personnel practices.

2. Making sure the company meets all the various Federal and State personnel laws such as E.E.O., etc.

3. Trying to find the best benefits package for the company's employees at the lowest price.

4. Maintaining all personnel records and mak-

ing sure the records and the employees behind the records are properly protected from the prying eyes of unauthorized individuals.

5. Keeping track of all vacation time, overtime, compensatory time and other earned benefits for every employee in the company.

6. Keeping track of pension funds, savings plans and other programs set up to help employees plan for their future.

7. Keeping track of payroll and all the deductions that must come out of each paycheck.

8. Hiring new employees.

Given these priorities, it is not surprising that dealing with human resources requires working with a different set of rules. In most cases, the rules are set up to protect the company. On occasion, the rules include a few requirements that give human resources more power than necessary and help ensure their job security. Who can blame them for that? Because of the legal concerns listed above, the personnel department's involvement in the hiring process is defensive innture. To address their concerns, they will insist on some or all of the following:

1. They do not want the company involved in a lawsuit with a recruiter. Therefore, they will insist that each recruiter send in resumés of the candidates they represent. Each resumé is immediately recorded in human resources, along with the time and date received. In the event that a second recruiter claims to represent the hired candidate, the human resource department has a record of who first represented the candidate to the company. They believe they can keep a second recruiter from suing by keeping these records.

2. They may want you to sign a contract agreeing to certain methods of representing candidates. Look over such a contract carefully. Some requirements are just procedural and basically innocuous. However, in trying to protect the company, some could place you in jeopardy. For instance, more than one company has tried to get me to sign an agreement stating that I would notify human resources if one of their employees contacted me about looking for a new position. This would be a violation of that employee's right to confidentiality and might be grounds for legal action against me by that employee.

3. Some human resource people look at recruiters as a necessary evil. They consider recruiters thieves who steal good employees from their company, then call back a few days later trying to get a commission for replacing the stolen person. Unfortunately, there are a few recruiters who are not above attempting this. However, no one can steal an employee who doesn't want to be stolen. As discussed earlier, changing employment is a big decision in most people's lives. They are not going to change positions just because a recruiter wants them to. If a company is losing good employees, it is because they aren't doing what is necessary to keep their employees.

Keeping all these things in mind, let's look at some of the objections you might get from someone in human resources.

Objection: "We don't use recruiters."

Interpretation: This situation is quite a bit different than when you were talking with the hiring manager. The objection is still a brush-off, however. Every company has an occasional position that can't be filled any other way. The difference between the manager and human resources may be in where the money comes from. Often, the direct expenses incurred in hiring a candidate comes out of personnel's budget. They will have allocated a certain amount of money for running ads, paying fees, etc., and they'll want to spend as little of this money as possible. The indirect costs of hiring someone are going to be of little concern to human resources. Those hidden costs are only going to impact the hiring manager.

Response: "I can understand that you would not want to pay a fee if at all possible. However, I'm not asking you to pay a fee at this time. Let me present you with some of my best candidates. If you like them well enough, you can decide at that time whether you want to pay a fee." (You may not want to work under such circumstances but, at least, the decision is yours, not theirs.)

Human resources is going to have all the same objections that the hiring manager had. For the most part, the same responses will apply. However, you must remember that the money for the recruiter's fee will most likely be coming out of human resources' budget. Therefore, finances will be their major concern, not whether the best candidate is hired or how much time it will take to hire someone. They will also be less concerned about the indirect costs of hiring. Protecting the company will be uppermost in their minds. Therefore, anything you say that will ease their concerns regarding possible lawsuits and infractions of EOE laws will help. Some of the things I say in an effort to alleviate their concerns include:

» "I will talk to all candidates before submitting them to you to be sure they have not heard about the position from any other source. I won't waste your time or mine by submitting a candidate who has not expressed an interest in the position, and I will instruct all candidates to tell any other recruiter who might call about the position that they are already being represented to your company."

» "Before recommending any candidate to you I will do some preliminary checks to be sure that the information I provide or that is found on their resumé is correct. You are probably aware of the current study in which it was discovered that nearly 80% of the resumés that candidates submit contain lies."

» "One of the main reasons I decided to specialize in this one small group of professionals was to make life less complicated for people like you. By working with a specialist, you don't need to work with a lot of agencies. Because I specialize, I will have in my database virtually every candidate the other agencies might offer. You can work with me alone and get the same candidates without the hassle or the legal concerns that might arise when working with multiple agencies."

» "I will not send you anyone you might pick up through your newspaper ad. In fact, I try to avoid representing those people. I do, after all, provide a guarantee for the people I place, and people who answer ads tend to be too unreliable for me to guarantee. They have a tendency to accept a position just for the income while they continue to look for the position they really want. I can't risk offering a guarantee on such candidates."

Objections you might get regarding fees and guarantees will be covered in Chapter 10.

SCHEDULING CALL BACKS

By the time you have completed your first call to a hiring manager and followed up on that call, you should have gathered enough basic information about the manager's area of responsibility to set up a schedule of future calls. You should have a pretty good idea of how many new positions the manager has budgeted for and when he will be looking for people to fill these positions. You also should have a pretty good idea of how many employees are in the manager's department or section. With this information you can plan a follow-up schedule that will not drive the manager crazy but will still get you in contact with the manager around the time a position is going to open up.

When dealing with a budgeted position, plan your contact call about two or three weeks before the manager actually anticipates opening up the position. If the manager is on schedule, this will give you several weeks to put together a group of good candidates to present the minute the position becomes available. If the vacancy is going to be delayed, confirm with the manager a call back time that is about two or three weeks before the next anticipated opening for the position. Occasionally, a position will open up earlier than anticipated. By calling three weeks early, you will catch this early opening.

Setting up a schedule for unanticipated openings requires a different approach. Since the manager is not expecting anyone to leave, you cannot establish a specific date to call back. However, you can set up a schedule based on two factors: the size and stability of the department or section. Size is easy to determine by asking the manager how many people work in the department. Stability can only be determined with time. As you continue to talk with people in the profession you have chosen to represent, you will learn about places that are great to work for and about places that are not so great to work for. This will determine, to some extent, a department's turnover rate.

In most professions, the average professional will change positions every two and one-half to three years (between a year and one-half to two years in sales). By looking at this figure in relation to the number of professionals working in a department, you can come up with a reasonable means of determining how many unanticipated openings there will be in a particular department during the year. For instance, if the accounting department of a company has twelve accountants, you can expect three of the accountants to move on during the course of the year. If the computer programming department has twenty employees, you can estimate that somewhere between five and six employees may move on during the year. In the first instance (with accountants), you should check in with the manager at least four times during the year. In the second instance (with programmers), you need to contact the manager at least six times during the course of the year. As you get more experienced, you can increase or decrease the number of calls based on the reputation of the department.

Later, we will discuss setting up a tickler file to keep track of call-back dates.

ABOUT EXCLUSIVES

We have talked quite a bit about getting "exclusive" search assignments. Let's look at the subject of exclusivity in greater detail to determine when and whether to get one. We'll also need to consider what advantages might accrue to the manager or human resource person who gave you an "exclusive."

One of the obvious advantages you get from having an exclusive search assignment is that the competition is eliminated. Having an exclusive arrangement, of course, means you have greatly increased your odds of filling the position and collecting the fee. In addition, if you do a good job, the manager is likely to turn to you again the next time there's a position to be filled.

However, you may not always *want* to go for an exclusive on a search assignment. Before making the commitment, you must be sure you can find enough candidates to give the manager a good group of people to chose from. Regardless of how good your candidate may be, few managers would be willing to make a hiring decision after interviewing just one or two candidates. Some companies even have a policy mandating that at least three or four candidates be evaluated before one can be hired. By accepting an exclusive, you are promising to find at least four good candidates. Should you ask for such an assignment and then not be able to fulfill your obligation, you might leave a bad taste in the manager's mouth. Having said that, I still recommend that you pursue an exclusive any time the position matches well with your database.

Obviously, the hiring manager is not going to give you an exclusive without realizing some benefit from the arrangement. Let's look at some of the concerns a manager might have about giving you an exclusive, then let's look at the benefits.

62

The biggest concern a manager will have about giving anyone an exclusive is that the recruiter will not have access to the very best available candidates. You need to address this issue even if the manager doesn't bring it up. It will be lurking somewhere in the back of the hiring manager's mind and, if not, some other recruiter is sure to bring it up. Often, the manager's perception will be that the more recruiters used, the more candidates will be contacted. This is simply not true. No recruiter has an exclusive database. Many of the good candidates in a particular profession will appear in several different recruiters' database. When handling this concern, first mention all the advantages the manager will reap by giving you an exclusive. Then explain why a concern about not seeing all the best candidates is unfounded. Here are the benefits a manager gains by giving you an exclusive.

1. The manager eliminates the risk of two recruiters trying to represent the same candidate. Although the manager may not realize it, when two different recruiters lay claim to the same person, that person cannot be hired by the manager unless he or she is willing to pay a full fee to both recruiters. (This can be easily avoided, as will be demonstrated later.)

2. The manager avoids being subjected to numerous, time-consuming phone calls. You can guarantee that the entire recruiting and hiring processes will be completed with a minimum of interruptions, because you will take care of all the arrangements. All the manager needs to do is interview the top four (or six) candidates.

3. By using one recruiter, the manager can be assured that the entire process will be han-

dled delicately and, when necessary, with the utmost confidentiality. Although this may not be a critical issue, it is still desirable to make the hiring process as low key as possible so as not to disturb the other members of the manager's team.

4. Although I don't normally recommend it, you can discount your fee for an exclusive. Make this offer based on the assumption that you have the fee in the bag and are willing to give the manager a small discount for such an assurance. I don't recommend this because the manager doesn't expect it, and why give away good money? In Chapter 10 we will discuss how to use your fee as a bargaining tool for bigger and better things. Don't give anything away here unless you have to.

In the process of pointing out the benefits the manager will gain by using just one recruiter, you will have taken some of the sting out of the concern about not seeing the very best candidates. However, I would still address this concern, even if it is never mentioned.

"I can understand how you might be concerned about missing some of the best candidates if you do not use additional recruiters. However, let me assure you that this will not happen. My network and my database cover the entire spectrum of professionals working in this field. If I was not absolutely sure you are going to get four (or six) top candidates, I would contact the other recruiters that specialize in this field myself."

Having said all this, I will now say that asking for an exclusive should be totally unnecessary. If you will recall what was discussed in

Chapter 2, you remember that we got ourselves an exclusive just by taking the search assignment correctly to begin with. Whenever you get a manager to agree to interview four or six people you have selected, at a place and time you have selected, you have the equivalent of an exclusive. The manager is not going to fool around with other recruiters when he or she is committed to interviewing four or six people. The other recruiters may continue to send in resumés, but they are not going to get any of their candidates interviewed, much less hired.

The only real purpose in talking to a manager about an exclusive is to help the manager avoid the hassle of dealing with a number of recruiters and encountering the problems we discussed above. If you can convince the hiring manager that you will produce four or six top-notch candidates, why bother dealing with a bunch of other recruiters?

Other than that, getting the manager to agree to an exclusive means very little. How are you going to enforce such an agreement? What are you going to do if you find out the manager is working with another recruiter? A verbal agreement from a manager, no matter how well intended, means very little. Your only real guarantee of getting an exclusive is to take charge of the hiring process and arrange to have the manager interview your four or six best candidates.

Many recruiters ask for an exclusive. On occasion, you will encounter a manager who will tell you that another recruiter has an exclusive. Generally, this means that the recruiter has not set up the hiring agreements or interview agreements discussed in Chapter 2. Without such agreements, the exclusive designation is

nothing more than an attempt to keep other recruiters away until the recruiter with the exclusive is able to come up with an acceptable candidate. This is of absolutely no benefit to the manager. When I run across such a situation, I immediately ask several questions.

"I can see where the exclusive would be of advantage to the recruiter. What benefit do you get from giving the recruiter an exclusive?"

Perhaps the manager will say a reduced fee was arranged in exchange for the exclusive. In which case, ask:

"How long does the exclusive run? What happens if the recruiter doesn't come up with any acceptable candidates within a reasonable time (like two weeks)?"

You can bet your bottom dollar that the manager will not have thought to put a time limit on the exclusive and that the recruiter didn't volunteer one. However, don't comment on this just yet. Let it lie there as food for thought as you proceed to the next question:

"Did you sign any sort of contract when you granted this recruiter an exclusive? What sort of penalty would you suffer if you violated the agreement? What sort of penalty would the recruiter suffer by violating the agreement?"

There is almost never a written contract, just a verbal request from the recruiter and a verbal agreement from the manager. However, every once in a while, a recruiter is smart enough to get the manager to sign a written agreement, but there is seldom a penalty for violating the contract. The only purpose the contract serves is to scare the manager from

CLIENT RECORD

Company _____

Phone _____ Fax _____

Address _____

City _____ State _____ Zip _____

Mailing Address _____

City _____ State _____ Zip _____

Manager _____ Title _____ Phone/ext. _____

Manager _____ Title _____ Phone/ext. _____

Manager _____ Title _____ Phone/ext. _____

Employees (potential recruits)

Name _____ Title _____ Phone _____

Name _____ Title _____ Phone _____

Name _____ Title _____ Phone _____

Name _____ Title _____ Phone _____

Name _____ Title _____ Phone _____

Miscellaneous _____

_____

_____

_____

_____

Fee _____ Guarantee _____

Code 1 _____

Code 2 _____

Code 3 _____

working with another recruiter. That's why I ask about the penalty. Only once in ten years have I seen a recruiter trap a manager into signing an agreement with a penalty in it. In this case, the manager agreed to pay the recruiter a fee if the manager hired anyone within the next six months regardless of the source of the candidate. The poor manager was trapped. Even if a well-qualified candidate walked through the door of the company and asked for a job, the manager would owe the recruiter a fee.

As you can see, when the above three questions are asked, everyone becomes aware that the exclusive agreement has no real substance. The only thing holding the agreement together is the manager's integrity and good will. Even integrity and good will erode when the manager discovers that he has given away everything and gotten nothing in return. However, I never put down a fellow recruiter or suggest that the manager violate an agreement. I merely make the following proposal: "Why don't I put together a back-up system for you, just in case the other recruiter isn't able to find enough good candidates within a reasonable time? I'm going to begin a search right now, so I'll have four very good candidates ready for you in case you need them. The other recruiter has been working on this assignment for two weeks now. If that person hasn't produced several strong candidates by this time next week, I'd guess that some unforeseen problems have come up. In all good conscience, I think we can look at the candidates I'll have available at that time without violating your agreement with the other recruiter. Incidentally, I will work for the same fee that the other recruiter was charging."

The *Client Record* form on page 65 will help you keep track of hiring managers and employees at a client company. Current employees are future candidates, and next chapter you'll learn how to recruit them.

On the Client Record form, note any specialized information about the company under **Miscellaneous.** For instance, if you work with computer programmers, you might want to note the computer system the company uses, the software installed there, the computer languages employed, and so forth.

Fees and Guarantees are discussed in detail in Chapter 10.

Codes can be used to sort companies by various characteristics. For instance, if you are dealing with sales people, you might choose to segment companies by the products they manufacture. If Code A were used for this purpose, 11 might stand for steel, 12 for aluminum, 13 for chrome, etc. Code B might be used to sort companies by location, with 21 representing the Midwest, for example. Code C might be used to identify the type of clients the products are sold to, automobile manufacturers, for example, or hospitals.

Used properly, these codes can simplify the process of matching a candidate to the company most likely to appreciate a candidate's experience and special talents. For example, you may have a candidate experienced in selling steel to automobile companies in Michigan. Any company in the same business, selling to the same clients, would be eager to interview your candidate because of his or her knowledge and contacts in the industry.

Now, let's get some good candidates for your data base.

CHAPTER 5

THE CANDIDATE

TIME IS THE COIN OF LIFE.
IT IS THE ONLY COIN YOU
HAVE, AND ONLY YOU
CAN DETERMINE HOW IT
WILL BE SPENT. BE CAREFUL
LEST YOU LET OTHER
PEOPLE SPEND IT FOR YOU.

— CARL SANDBURG

You can choose to work with a profession where search assignments are relatively easy to come by, or you can choose a profession where candidates are relatively easy to come by, or you can choose something in between, but no matter how you slice it there's going to be some kind of a trade off. We've looked at all the problems you might face in getting search assignments, so even where they are almost impossible to get, you're still going to get more than your share, because of the *way* you work. In the next three chapters, we're going to apply the same basic philosophy to finding candidates. If you embrace this philosophy, you'll be successful whether you select a profession where finding search assignments is the greater challenge or whether you select an area where *finding candidates* is the greater challenge.

One of the things that makes recruiting different from almost any other business is that you must manage two different databases and dovetail them together almost perfectly. We've already discussed how to build a large database of client companies (and the hiring managers within these companies who will hire the professionals you represent). Now you're going to build a proper database of professional candidates to fill vacant positions in your client companies.

WHO IS THE CANDIDATE?

It's important to recognize who should and who should *not* be in your database. We've talked at length about the danger of accepting a search assignment outside your area of specialization. Working with a candidate outside your specialized area can be equally destructive, but there will be times when you are going to be very tempted to do so.

Not long ago, I met some software engineers highly skilled in modifying UNIX kernels who were looking for a recruiter to help them find new positions. I knew that talent like theirs was always in demand. Engineers of this caliber are almost certain placements for a recruiter. In my earlier years, I would have clutched these rare finds to my bosom and immediately launched an all-out search for appropriate companies and hiring managers. I might have even placed one of them. Later, I would have realized how much it cost me to make that placement.

The costs of going astray are not always apparent. There are a multitude of hidden costs in recruiting, just as there are in the hiring process. When you work with a candidate outside your area of specialization, you can't maintain continual contact with people in your area of specialization, and this is essential to your success. While you are chasing the rainbow in a field you know very little about, two or three very lucrative search assignments can slip by unnoticed in your area of specialization.

In the recruiting business, good time management is essential. There are only so many working hours in a day and they need to be used wisely or you will begin to fall behind. When you fall behind, you stop exercising good judgment. Before you know it, you start grasping at anything that comes along and eventually find yourself in the same market as recruiting agencies. You will start working on those sixty-to-one shots and sending resumés to human resources departments. Pretty soon, your income will be reduced to that of an employee in a recruiting agency. The better you are at managing your time, the better your income will be. That's why you should always spend your time finding search assignments where your odds of filling them are three out of four.

The same principals hold true in working with candidates. Within any professional area you'll find a variety of different skills and experience levels. You need to identify where the greatest demand lies, and focus there. This is going to be difficult at first, but experience will help you refine your database. In every profession, some candidates are considered *golden,* because you can almost guarantee placement. Golden candidates differ a little from profession to profession, but they all share these universal qualities:

1. *A Bachelor's or Master's Degree from a recognized college or university with a major in their chosen profession.* Every hiring manager is attracted to a candidate with a degree. The degree is a sign that the individual is

able to accept a challenge and stick with it to completion. A degree from a recognized school indicates that the candidate received a good education and was properly challenged. Managers feel that getting a degree in one's chosen field means the candidate is career-focused. Every manager wants candidates who know what they want and are not afraid to go after it. They like motivated candidates.

2. *Two to three years of working experience in the chosen profession.* Although it might seem logical that the more experience a candidate has the more attractive he or she is, but this is not true for several reasons. First, every department is made up of few managers and many workers. There's always going to be approximately six times as many positions available for engineers, programmers, accountants or salespeople than there will be for managers or supervisors. Besides, internal promotions are often the case when companies have openings for managers or supervisors. On the other hand, companies can't fill staff positions through internal promotions. Therefore, the demand for worker bees is twenty times higher than for candidates eligible for supervisor/manager positions. Second, someone with about two or three years experience has enough experience to be a competent professional but is not far enough along careerwise to expect a promotion in the near future. Therefore, that employee is going to stay in the new position much longer. People with four, five or six years of experience are either about ready to take on supervisory responsibilities or they are duds. Finally, people with two to three years of experience are bargains.

They bring a lot of skills to their new positions but not big salary requirements. As you will recall, when we were discussing salaries with the hiring manager, we learned that the person most apt to meet the functional and salary requirements of a position was someone on the way up, not someone already there. Every hiring manager would like to hire someone with around two or three years of experience.

3. *A person with an outgoing personality.* Most professionals are required to meet with and work with other people, and most managers will associate an outgoing personality with an ability to work well with other people. Hiring managers believe their employees are a reflection on their departments and always want their departments well represented. Managers feel that an employee with an outgoing personality makes a better impression on people outside the department. Although this is not necessarily true, it is the perception and you must react to it. Personable candidates also interview much better.

A good recruiter always recognizes golden candidates and doesn't let them go to waste. Sharp recruiters market the candidate to their clients first. That is, they call all their clients and let the clients know they have someone special. If the candidate is good, the recruiter will find several managers interested in seeing the person even though they have no official opening. Many managers have the flexibility of creating a position if the right person comes along.

Before marketing a golden candidate, I establish a reasonable fee for the candidate and let each manager know what the fee will be.

69

The manager will know if he or she can afford to hire the candidate, and nobody's time is wasted. I also tell the managers there is a set fee for the candidate so no one will accuse me of creating a bidding war between the managers of various companies. In this way, the candidate can make a decision about which company to work for without any pressure from me. I get the same fee regardless of whom the candidate chooses to work for. I have always found a company that was interested in hiring my golden candidates.

Unfortunately, golden candidates are relatively rare and our database would be very small if we only stocked it with golden candidates. Hiring managers know this and will accept less than absolutely perfect candidates because they know they could wait a long time for a golden person. Therefore, you'll be able to place many professionals in your area of specialization who are not golden. However, the further removed from golden, the more difficult it will be to place a candidate. Your ability to exercise good judgment is once again a major asset, because you must differentiate the professionals you can place from those you cannot. A database full of unplaceable candidates is absolutely useless.

Here are some basic rules of thumb to follow in developing your database:

1. Don't spend time trying to place supervisors and managers. Treat them with respect, however. While you won't be placing them, they may hire from you in the future.

2. Cultivate entry level people and people with limited experience. They will become golden candidates after they've had two years of experience.

3. Be wary of professionals with many years of experience who are willing to take a low salary. Their competency is going to be suspect. Check their references carefully before you consider representing them.

4. Don't overlook shy or introverted professionals. They are often the best workers. When representing these people, make sure they are accompanied by strong, positive references and they will be sure placements. These candidates appreciate good recruiters because the recruiter can represent them more accurately than they can represent themselves.

FINDING THE CANDIDATES

As with search assignments, there are a lot of candidates out there if you know where to look for them. Let's start with the obvious places.

In the Departments

Workers in every department of every company are potential candidates: accountants in every accounting department, doctors in every hospital, metal salespersons in every metals company, etc. Not every company will be your client, by your choice or theirs. Not every company will be interested in working your way, and you in turn will not be interested in working with companies that insist upon resumés being sent to human resource departments.

You can still recruit from companies you do not work with. Recruiting is discussed in detail next chapter.

Newspaper want ads

Many of your clients have found good candidates by running want ads in the newspaper, and you can do likewise. However, you will gain far more from the want ad than the client. The client runs an ad for just one purpose: to fill a position. The recruiter runs an ad for several purposes: to fill an existing position, to get candidates for future positions, and to find resources that will lead other candidates. Every candidate you pick up from your newspaper want ad will have information for you. This information might include the names of other candidates that the respondent has been working with and locations of search assignments that have not panned out. Remember, anyone who answers your want ad has used other resources to find a position. Also remember that this person has been working alongside other people who possess the same professional skills. All this information can be yours if you go about it right. We will discuss how to get this information in Chapter 7.

You need to take some precautions when running an ad. You are going to get many resumés from people who are not appropriate candidates for your database. In fact, only about one in every five or ten respondents will be a good candidate. It's important to recognize with whom to spend time and to avoid the temptation to spend time with people who don't belong in your database, *i.e., people you will never place.*

When running an ad, you must comply with two rules:

» You must have a position to fill that meets the specifications described in the ad.

» You must acknowledge every response you get. Human resource departments at most companies and recruiting agencies employ a form letter that automatically goes out the second a resume is received. It's probably wise for you to adopt this practice as well.

Make your ad simple. When your clients run an ad, they generally include as many specifics about the position as possible in an attempt to screen out unqualified people. If you're unfamiliar with how companies run their ads, study the want ads placed by companies in your area of specialization. They are generally wordy, detailed and quite expensive. Your purpose, however, is to attract as many good candidates as possible, regardless of whether they fit a position you currently have open. Although there may be a lot of requirements for the position you want to fill, avoid putting anything in the ad that would allow a candidate who fits your database from self-disqualification. Many things can go into the ad, but the only thing critical is the type of person you are looking for. In other words, you must note that you are looking for an accountant, an engineer a salesperson, or whatever. Everything beyond that is optional. Salary, location, type of company, skills needed, experience required, duties, responsibilities, and other details should be included only if they do not disqualify candidates for your database. For instance, putting the location of the position will eliminate all those candidates not interested in working there. If you want to eliminate those candidates, fine, but it won't help you build your database nearly so fast.

Referrals

In time, this will be one of your best methods of adding to your database. That's why I always make it known I'm looking for a certain type of professional, no matter whom I'm talking with. I come in contact with a lot of unqualified people, through my ad or through other resources; however, I don't just dismiss them. I explain to them that I specialize in a certain area and, for that reason, won't be of much help to them. And I try to refer them to someone who can help them. If possible, I try to refer them to a recruiter who specializes in placing people with their background. You'd be surprised how often I'm rewarded for making such a referral. A recruiter who strings a candidate along is doing neither the candidate nor the recruiter a favor. The candidate is left with false hopes, and the recruiter will wind up with an undesirable reputation.

Everyone in your database is in contact with others who should also be in your database. However, most people are reluctant to reveal the names of their peers, assuming that most people don't want their names given to a recruiter. In some cases this is true. Therefore, you need to provide some assurances to people you are hoping to get referrals from. First and foremost, assure them that their confidentiality will be respected. Make sure they understand that you will never reveal the source of any information you receive from them without their permission. Second, you need to assure your sources that people you contact will benefit. I usually advise my sources that I will offer their peers the opportunity to learn what I know is happening in the marketplace. These peers can then decide whether or not they wish to take advantage of the program I have to offer. Finally, I advise my sources that people have the right to make their own decisions. If they fail to give me the names of their peers, they have, in effect, made a "no" decision on

behalf of these peers. In so doing they have deprived these peers of the opportunity of making the decision for themselves.

Interviews

If you are interviewing the right people, you will always be interviewing someone working with the very professionals you want for your database. We'll study the interviewing process in detail in Chapter 7 and discuss how to identify the professionals you want to recruit.

References

In Chapter 8, we'll discuss references. For now, note that if the candidate providing references is placeable, those references may well be people you want in your database.

Professional Societies

There is probably no better place to get acquainted with placeable candidates than through membership in a professional society that caters to the individuals you represent. As I mentioned earlier, most good recruiters are very active in these organizations and often serve as officers. A smart recruiter might volunteer to be membership chairman of one of these organizations. What a wonderful excuse for staying in contact with the people in your database and for asking for the names of other professionals who might be interested in joining the organization. You will be amazed at the number of referrals you will start to get once you are a well-known member of such an organization.

Company Phone Directories

Most companies have some sort of internal

phone directory that lists the name of all employees, their department, their phone number, and their title. Intended for internal use only, they are usually closely guarded. However, disgruntled employees are sometimes willing to leave a directory in the hands of their favorite recruiter when asked. The directories of very large companies, in which the various departments are so large that employees know only the people in their own small group, are particularly valuable. For instance, I know of one company that has over 1500 programmers in their M.I.S. department and over 1000 accountants in their accounting department. A programmer or accountant in this company probably knows fewer than twenty out of these 1000 or 1500 possible recruits. When you have possession of the directory, you'll know about all of them.

PREPARING FOR THE INTERVIEW

Very few people know how to prepare for an interview. This is not surprising, since most of us are interviewed only a few times during our entire lives. However, those who have the best interviewing skills generally land the jobs they interview for, regardless of whether they are the best applicants. Conversely, many good, highly skilled candidates are passed over because they do not interview well. This is bad news for the companies and the candidates they erroneously reject. Fortunately, recruiters can alleviate this inequity and provide an important service to the entire hiring industry as well as to their clients.

When a recruiter selects four or six candidates for the hiring manager to interview, the recruiter does not select them on the basis of their interviewing skills. Rather, the recruiter selects them based on reference checks, so they have the best work ethic and best skills, and were most admired in their previous positions. Just because they were outstanding in their previous employment, however, doesn't mean that the candidates will do well in an interview.

A good recruiter overcomes a manager's interviewing prejudice by preparing candidates thoroughly for the interview. Prepared properly, your candidates will stand head and shoulder above candidates from other sources. Most candidates will appreciate any help you can give them, and here are some ways you can prepare your candidates:

1. *Make sure they are well informed.* Familiarize your candidate with the company and the position. The person interviewing your candidate will be very impressed by the time it appears your candidate spent researching the company before coming for the interview. Your candidate should be able to tell the interviewer exactly why he or she selected this particular company.

2. *Make sure they are well dressed.* Regardless of the company's dress code, your male candidates should wear a conservative suit, white shirt and conservative tie. Female candidates should wear a nice suit or a skirt with a conservative blouse and a jacket. Perfume should be used sparingly.

3. *Help them evaluate themselves.* Have each candidate write down their perceived strengths and accomplishments and be prepared to talk about them. Encourage them to be ready to respond to the following questions:

   a)   Tell me about yourself.

b) Why are you interested in this company?

c) Why are you leaving your current position?

d) Why should we hire you?

e) What are your long range goals?

f) What are your greatest strengths?

g) What are your greatest weaknesses?

h) Tell me about your previous boss and company.

i) What's important to you in a job?

j) What do you do in your spare time?

k) How would others describe you?

l) Tell me about your educational background.

m) What was least enjoyable about your last job?

n) What do you dislike most about the person you report to?

o) What is outstanding about you?

p) Why should you be hired?

q) What can you contribute to the organization?

4. Help candidates prepare a list of questions to ask the interviewer. Make sure each candidate writes these questions down and places them in a folder to be carried to the interview. The interviewer will be extremely impressed that the candidate came so well prepared. Some possible questions are:

a) What will you expect of me?

b) Which of my special talents could be useful?

c) What are the goals and time frames to complete the job?

d) What is the structure of the organization above and below you?

e) What strategy does the company have for growth?

f) How does management view the department?

g) Where do you see this position leading?

h) If you were promoted, would it be expected that I would take over your current responsibilities?

5. Make sure candidates plan to arrive ten minutes early. This will give them time to check their appearance and go over their notes. Tell them to go into the interview with confidence. Instruct them to carry a portfolio to the interview and open it at the beginning so they can jot down notes and refer to the questions they have prepared.

6. Make sure they are prepared to fill out an application. Tell them to carry a resumé with them so they can put the correct dates on the application. Conflicting dates always raise concerns. If references are asked for, they should put them down; however, they should never volunteer references. You, the recruiter, would rather provide the reference checks.

7. As a rule, interviewers extend their hand and introduce themselves first. However, candidates should be aware that the interviewer may not respond in this way. Therefore, they should know that if the interviewer doesn't extend a hand right away, the candidate should do it. Be sure the hand shake is firm but not a death grip. This is expected of women as well as men. Limp handshakes are a turn-off.

8. Candidates should not decide where to sit. They must wait until the interviewer indicates where they should sit before making a move.

9. Body language is extremely important. Tell your candidate to be themselves; however, most interviewers want candidates to show some enthusiasm about the position. Therefore, candidates should sit forward in their chairs while expressing sincere interest. As they listen to the position described, they should jot down anything they have previously done that complements the position. They should mention these points before the interview is concluded.

10. Candidates should ask for the position at the end of the interview. Even if they are not sure they want the job they should ask for it, just in case. The only time they should not ask for it is if they are sure they don't want it. If there is some uncertainty, they can make a better decision after a second interview. Encourage the candidate to practice ending the interview with a positive statement, choosing words that assume that an offer is forthcoming. For example:

"I'm really interested in the position we've been discussing. I like your company, and I feel I can bring a lot to your organization. I'd like to come back and speak with you further. When can we get together?"

11. The candidate should be discouraged from talking about compensation. The recruiter should encourage both the hiring manager and the candidate to avoid discussing this issue. This is something that you, the recruiter, should be negotiating on behalf of both of them. (This subject will be thoroughly discussed in Chapter 9.) There is no good way to ask the question (for example, If the hiring manager were to ask, "What sort of salary were you looking for?" it would cast the company in an unattractive light). However, answering the question is even worse. Obviously, candidates want just as much as possible, but they don't want to eliminate themselves from contention by asking for too much. If the situation should arise, the candidate should be instructed to answer along the following lines:

"The recruiter indicated that this position was within the salary range I'm looking for. Besides, I'm more interested in an opportunity. I'm sure if this position is right for me, you'll make an offer I'll be pleased to accept."

Now, let's learn how to recruit some very good candidates. candidates who will wait for your direction because you took the time to work out some agreements with them.

CHAPTER 6

RECRUITING

THE SUCCESSFUL PERSON IS SOMEBODY WHO HAS INTEGRITY AND IS CONSISTENT.

Many recruiters have told me that they don't like to recruit and I've always found this rather strange. To me, recruiting has always been much easier than marketing for search assignments. Then, when I started teaching the art of recruiting, I learned why some people have trouble recruiting. Recruiters who have trouble have no idea what they have to offer a candidate. Obviously, if they have nothing to offer a potential candidate, recruiting will be tough.

What You Offer Candidates

You have much to offer good candidates, and you both need to acknowledge the mutuality of your relationship. For example, you offer:

1. *Job security.* Workers assume that their company and their position will be there forever. They think that buy-outs, bankruptcies and layoffs only happen to other people. There is no guarantee, however, of

job security with any company, anywhere. No company would be willing to sign a contract offering an employee a position until retirement, even if an employee were willing to sign a contract stating that he or she would stay until retirement. The bottom line is, companies can no longer offer job security. Workers must take responsibility for their own job security.

Job security for a professional consists of three things:

» Maintaining functional competency. That is, making sure that one's technical, managerial and interpersonal skills are always current;

» Being aware of the market value of one's skills, talents, and experience;

» Maintaining ongoing visibility in the marketplace, both inside and outside the place of current employment.

Candidates who work full time have little time or opportunity to carry out these activities. They have neither the time nor the opportunity to determine what new technologies and innovations are occurring in other companies. They have neither the time nor the ability to assess the value of their skills, talents and experience in the current market. And they certainly do not have the time or the contacts with the marketplace outside their own company to maintain visibility.

A recruiter, on the other hand, is in constant contact with the marketplace. Recruiters know what skills are in demand at other companies and how much those companies are willing to pay for a particular level of experience, skills and ability. Most important, a recruiter can always keep a candidate informed of what is

taking place in the marketplace. Candidates should consider recruiters as an extremely valuable resource; however, most candidates are not aware of this. They need to be made aware that a good relationship with a recruiter is their very best form of job security.

2. *Career Planning*. Few professionals have the time or opportunity to plan their careers. They may have some vague idea about how they are going to advance within their current company, but this is hardly a career plan. Planning any career around a company that may not even be there tomorrow is fraught with danger. No professional can hope to develop a decent career plan without the assistance of a recruiter.

For a professional, planning a career involves setting up a series of short-term and long-term goals, and then entering into a series of agreements with a recruiter. Later, we'll talk about the candidate's *Reason For Leaving* (RFL). Whenever possible, try to ensure that the candidate's reason for leaving the current position is linked with his or her career plan.

Both parties are responsible for making sure that the candidate's career plan is carried out. The candidate is responsible for continuing to learn new skills and for gaining new experiences. The recruiter is responsible for keeping the candidate aware of the marketplace and of opportunities that will enhance the candidate's career.

3. *Confidante*. Things within a company are never stable, and some changes are sure to impact candidates. Most of the time, candidates view change negatively. For example, the people over them usually have the

greatest impact in determining how candidates enjoy their job. If employees don't like who they are working for, they won't stay very long. If they like who they are working for they'll be reluctant to leave. When a well liked boss is replaced, most professionals get very jittery.

Regardless of changes, candidates need someone objective with whom they can discuss their problems and review their possible options. Candidates should see the recruiter in this light, as their advocate in the event things turn from good to bad in their current work environment.

Sometimes I will get a call from a candidate who says, "Get me out of here!" Unfortunately, the candidate waited until conditions became unbearable before deciding to do something about it. It then becomes my task to try to keep the candidate from jumping from the frying pan into the fire. Candidates under this kind of pressure are likely to accept the first position that comes along, a position that may turn out to be worse than the one they are trying to escape. I try to get them to grit their teeth and stay with their present job until I can find them something that is not going to lead to further problems. Hopefully, I will find them a position that will be a positive move in terms of career growth.

Candidates who feel uncomfortable in their present situation should be willing to let you begin a low key search on their behalf. This might entail nothing more than watching for a position that will enhance their career. Most important, however, they need to be responsive to your suggestions and your evaluation of the situation. Don't let them become desperate before you and the candidate get se-

rious about finding him or her a new position.

RECRUITING THE CANDIDATE

If you've been conscientious in following my suggestions for accumulating potential candidates, you're soon going to have quite a list of names. Now let's recruit them. This won't be difficult if you remember what you have to offer.

The problem with most recruiters is that they don't contact potential candidates until a position opens. Nothing shakes up potential candidates more than to have someone call them out of the blue and offer them a new position. Unless a candidate is absolutely desperate to leave a current position, the answer is always going to be "No." After hearing "no" a few times, the recruiter decides that recruiting is tough. That's because the recruiter never actually recruited the candidate.

Look at it from the candidate's point of view. Unless a candidate is actively looking for another position, the candidate's focus will be on his or her present job and company. When recruiters call to talk about other positions, candidates feel threatened. Are they being asked to reject their current situation for something about which nothing is known? This is tantamount to calling strangers up and suggesting that they divorce their mates and marry people they've never even met. Of course, recruiters don't think that's what they're doing, but that's how candidates will view it. What you must understand is that moving a candidate from point A to point B is a gradual process. The good recruiter helps the candidate take it a step at a time. Changing positions requires a complete change in how the present job is perceived and how a new position is regarded.

With this in mind, let's recruit a candidate. On the next page you'll find a copy of the form I use for gathering information about a candidate. This form fits on a standard five by seven card or on a computer screen. So, let's assume you're going to recruit an accountant by the name of Jane Roe. Your name is John Doe and you got her name through one of Jane's associates. All you have is her work number, and you've already entered this information on the form.

Jane: "Hello. This is Jane."

John: "Jane Roe?" *(Always verify who you are talking to. Nothing is more embarrassing than to discover halfway through your presentation that you are talking to the wrong person.)*

Jane: "Yes."

John: "Jane, my name is John Doe. A friend thought it might be mutually beneficial if we got acquainted. I apologize for calling you at work. I hope I'm not calling at a real bad time."

At this point, she may want to know the friend's name. If so, I just say that I didn't ask the mutual friend if it was all right to give out his or her name. I assume that all information is given to me in confidence, and I won't break this bond of confidentiality without the other person's permission. I then offer to call my source to determine if it is all right to disclose that person's name. No one has ever asked me to do that. The prospective recruit respects the fact that I won't divulge a source without permission. Potential recruits feel much more comfortable talking with me when they know I will respect a confidence.

Jane: "What is this all about?"

John: "I'm a personnel consultant who works only with accountants with backgrounds similar to yours. Basically, I try to learn a little bit about who they are and what their career goals might be, and then I periodically keep them informed of anything that might be of interest in the marketplace. I know it must be very uncomfortable for you to talk at work. Would it be all right if I called you at home some evening so I can tell you more about who I am and what I'm all about?"

Jane: "I suppose so."

John: "Great. What's your home phone number?"

Jane: "734-9991, area code 592." *(Write it down on the form.)*

John: "What time is a good time to call? What time do you usually finish dinner and get the kids to bed?"

Jane: "Oh, around 8:30 or so."

John: "That sounds good. Why don't I give you a call tonight?"

Jane: "Okay."

CANDIDATE FILE

First _____ Last _____

Address _____

City _____ Zip _____

Phone (home) _____ Phone (work) _____

Current Employer _____

Title _____ Dates _____ Salary _____

Previous Employer _____

Title _____ Dates _____ Salary _____

Previous Employer _____

Title _____ Dates _____ Salary_ _____

Previous Employer _____

Title _____ Dates _____ Salary _____

Special Skills _____
_____

Personal Info _____
_____

Resumé _____ Last Update _____ Code _____

This call is totally non-threatening. I have not mentioned, or even hinted, that there might be a job change in her future. That is something we will agree upon later, when the time is right. However, I will start planning for it when I call her that evening. Let's jump to that call now.

John: "Hi, Jane. This is John Doe, the fellow who called you this afternoon at work. I hope I'm calling at a good time."

Jane: "This is fine."

John: "I promised you I'd tell you more about myself and what I do. As I mentioned earlier, I restrict my activities to working only with individuals with accounting backgrounds. I also only work with people who are referred to me. If I had to define my relationship to people like yourself, I would probably say that I view myself as their primary source for assuring that they always have job security. I help them follow whatever career path they might choose. Does that make sense to you?"

Jane: "I'm afraid I don't understand."

John: "I'm sorry. I have a habit of going way too fast. Let me explain what I mean about job security."

I now explain exactly what I mean by job security, using the same concepts we discussed earlier in this chapter. I point out why she cannot depend on her company to provide her with job security and why she must take on this responsibility herself. I then identify the three things that can guarantee her job security and how I can help in this regard. From here, I can move on to the concept of career planning.

John: "How long have you been working as an accountant for XYZ Company?"

Jane: "About two and a half years."

John: "Had you worked anywhere else as an accountant before joining XYZ Company?"

Jane: "No. This is my first job as an accountant. I used to wait tables while I was going to college."

John: "Have you given any thought to how you might use your two and a half years of experience as part of your overall career development?"

Jane: "No, not really."

John: "It's never to early to start thinking about it."

At this point you need to make a decision. You want to start helping Jane plan her career (including her next move). If you feel she is a very good candidate (maybe even a golden candidate), you should invite her to meet with you at her convenience so you can discuss the matter in person. Personal contacts always cement a relationship. If you have a current search assignment for which she is a perfect fit, you may want to meet with her regardless of whether she is better than the average candidate.

John: "I have some time next week, and some ideas that I'm sure you're going to be very happy with. Why don't we plan on getting together next week? Would Wednesday afternoon around four o'clock fit with your schedule?"

Should you determine that Jane is a good candidate but not someone you want to meet with at this time, you can continue the process over the phone. However, depending on time, it may take more than one phone call to complete all the agreements you'd like.

CAREER PLANNING

Career planning involves the development of a number of agreements between you and the candidate. Essentially, it consists of two things: the candidate's long term career expectations and the short term steps needed to get there. In most professions there are generally three career paths: *management, technical,* or *consulting.*

Management involves learning to oversee projects and, eventually, people. You'll be surprised at the number of professionals who do not want to deal with the headaches of managing other professionals.

Technical paths appeal to workers who aren't interested in interacting with lots of other people. Generally, these professionals are fascinated with the technical aspects of the business and are often referred to as gurus.

Consultants are the entrepreneurial members of the profession. Independent, they lend their expertise to any company willing to meet their price. As a rule, a consultant needs a few of the management skills and a lot of the technical skills; however, this varies from person to person and from profession to profession. It won't take you long to find out what your particular profession looks for in a consultant.

The first thing a candidate needs to decide is which career path to follow. This may be rather traumatic for someone with just a few years' experience. Assure anyone unwilling to commit that the decision is not irreversible. For instance, if a candidate opts for the managerial track, then is turned off by what a manager has to put up with, the preparation for management will not be lost. Most of what is learned along the path to becoming a manager will also be applicable to becoming a consultant or a technician.

Practically speaking, the preparation required for pursuing any of the career paths is about the same for the first four or five years. During those formative years, what's important is to learn as much as possible about the profession and business in general. Therefore, the recruiter and the candidate must work together to find the best working environment for the candidate, usually a work situation that is stimulating and provides many opportunities for learning new things.

Earlier, I alluded to the fact that the average stay for professionals in one position before moving to another position is two to three years. Two factors contribute to this phenomenon: salary and learning opportunities. During the first two or three years a professional is in a particular environment, many things that contribute to career growth are learned. Thereafter, learning opportunities begin diminishing rapidly. During this same two or three year period, one's salary increases at a steady rate. It may not sound like a handicap, but while learning opportunities continue to diminish, salary continues its gradual rise, and before long the professional will be unable to compete effectively in the job market. Salary requirements will exceed that of others with comparable skills. In order to compete in the marketplace, the professional will need to take a salary cut.

But even this creates problems.

A professional with six years' experience earning what professionals with only three years of experience earn looks bad. People who don't take advantage of learning opportunities when they become available severely damage their careers. This frequently means moving to a new position and a new company. If your candidate doesn't totally understand this, tell the story of John X.

John had been working as an accountant in the same department for ten years. As the person with the greatest longevity, he was certain he would be promoted when a new supervisory position became available. Much to his chagrin, a person with only six years experience was offered the position. Perplexed, John went to see the department manager to find out why he was bypassed for the promotion.

"Why," John asked, "would you promote someone with only six years' experience when I have ten years of experience?"

"Because," came the answer, "he had six years' experience. You, on the other hand, have had two years of experience repeated five times."

Once the candidate understands why it is important to plan for the future, you are ready to take the next step in the planning process: determining what the next position should offer. At this point, you are ready to establish a reason for leaving the current position and establishing a set of agreements with the candidate.

REASON FOR LEAVING

These three little words will recur frequently from now on. If you are one of those rare recruiters who takes the time to establish a relationship with all the candidates in your database, you will have a "Reason For Leaving" or RFL for each one, assuming, of course, that all the people in your database are placeable candidates. You don't want to set up this agreement with candidates who are not placeable.

Remember how we set up several agreements with a hiring manager? These agreements were designed to guarantee that you, rather than some other recruiter, would fill any position the manager had open. The RFL is basically a series of agreements between you and a candidate that will practically guarantee that you, rather than some other recruiter, will place the candidate.

Regardless of how happy a person is with a current position, there is always something that can be improved upon. It is up to you to discover what things are important to your candidates and which of these important things is lacking in their current positions. Once you've discovered this you've found a candidate's RFL. When you come upon a search assignment that responds positively to the things lacking in a candidate's current position, you have a placement.

On the next page, you'll find a form that will help you to determine the agreements you might make with a candidate. Once the form is completed, it should remain in the candidate's file. This form is designed to help candidates evaluate their current employment situation. It will help you identify the candidate's Reason For Leaving.

CANDIDATE AGREEMENTS

Reason For Leaving (RFL)

_____

_____

_____

CANDIDATE PRIORITIES

	Potential employer: Rate 0 to 5 with 0 = of no importance 5 = very important	Current employer: Rate 0 to 5 with 0 = very poor 5 = very good
1. Working environment	_____	_____
2. Career growth potential	_____	_____
3. Type of business	_____	_____
4. Learning opportunities	_____	_____
5. State-of-art technology	_____	_____
6. Training opportunities	_____	_____
7. Quality of your peers	_____	_____
8. Other working relationships	_____	_____
9. Quality of supervision	_____	_____
10. Size of company	_____	_____
11. Commute (location)	_____	_____
12. Employee benefits	_____	_____
13. Annual compensation	_____	_____

Location(s) _____

Annual compensation_____

Other priorities _____

Times available for interviews _____

RFL

The very first item on the form is RFL. Fill this out *after* you've helped the candidate evaluate his or her priorities. It will serve as your overall agreement with the candidate as to those conditions that are of sufficient importance for the candidate to move on to a new position and a new company. It is placed at the top of the form for easy reference, so it can be compared with search assignments as you receive them.

Candidate Priorities

Here are thirteen items that you will want to discuss with your candidate. Find out how important each is to him or her. Rate each issue from zero to five, with zero indicating that the candidate doesn't care about a particular issue and five indicating that the candidate considers the issue extremely important. In the same manner, find out how well the candidate's current position addresses each issue, so that a zero would indicate that his or her current position does not address this issue at all well and a five would mean that the issue is addressed extremely well.

Here are some guidelines for evaluating the relative importance of the thirteen qualities that a current employer may or may not possess, along with the qualities that a candidate might look for in considering a new situation.

Potential Employer

0 Not at all important

1 Very low on the candidate's list of priorities

2 Not important enough to impact a decision to accept another position or to leave the current position

3 Important enough to impact a decision about accepting another position or staying in a current position.

4 Very important. Would not accept a position that lacked the item and would accept another position where the issue was better addressed.

5 Extremely important. Would not consider a position that lacked the item and would leave any position where the issue was poorly addressed.

Current Employer Ratings

0 Present position doesn't address this issue at all.

1 Current position makes scant reference to this item. If the candidate considers this item important, he or she would leave their current position for this reason alone, all other things being equal.

2 The current position is substandard in this regard. Candidate would consider another position if this is an important item to him or her.

3 Current position addresses the issue adequately but not exceptionally.

4 Current position has almost everything in this regard. Few employers offer as much or more.

5 The current position has everything that could be hoped for in this regard. No other employer will match it. Most of the thirteen items on the Priorities List are self explanatory. Some, however, could use some clarification.

Working Environment: This is a general category but could include something you consider unimportant (the candidate who hates his small desk), or very important (the candidate who suffers from a complete lack of privacy). Never overlook any item addressed here. Some people judge their value to a company by comparing their desk with the size and placement of others'. It's not up to you to decide what's important but to take advantage of what's important to your candidate. If you can get a placement fee by finding a candidate a better desk in another company, so be it.

Career Growth Potential: Larger companies generally provide more opportunities for career growth internally because their departments are larger, so more supervisory positions will be available. This can also create problems for the candidate down the line because a supervisory position may be in one very specialized area. Later on, the candidate may need to demonstrate a solid involvement with all aspects of the profession to achieve further advancement. If career growth is an important issue, the candidate should probably be advised to move to a smaller department where there is an opportunity to experience all aspects of the profession.

Type of Business: Often this will rank as either a zero or a five in the candidate evaluation. Some people have moral objections to working for certain types of companies, such as companies that have an affiliation with the military, or companies that they perceive as having an adverse affect on the environment. People with strong feelings about such issues are often hard to place because they would rather work in unpleasant surroundings than betray their moral beliefs.

Learning Opportunities: This, too, is a general category. I view it as the opportunity to learn more about business, the profession, management, and other non technical issues.

State-of-the-art Technology: Future technocrats and consultants who need advanced technical exposure will see this as very important. They need to move to environments that herald the most current technical advances.

Training Opportunities: This may appear to duplicate the two preceding categories, but there are some basic differences. The aforementioned categories address the current environment within the company. The individual entering that environment can learn all the new things this environment has to offer. Training opportunities offer an opportunity to get training outside the company. Trainees will then bring these new ideas and technologies to the company and train others within the company.

Quality of Peers: Believe it or not, this can exert a major influence on a person's decision to change jobs. Working in close proximity to others day in and day out can prove frustrating if co-workers are difficult to get along with. I have had many calls from candidates requesting that I find them a new situation because of someone they found intolerable. Candidates who give this a five or four on the looking for side have probably experienced something like this.

Other Working Relationships: Most professionals are required to work with many other people besides those in their immediate group. These other relationships can have a big impact on their decision to stay where they are.

Quality of Supervision: The inability to tolerate their immediate supervisor is the most frequent reason people search for another job. What's worse than being underling to a person you can't respect or get along with? Make sure you ask this question correctly. Don't ask how the candidates get along with (or like) their immediate supervisor, because they won't give you an honest answer. Ask them how important it is to have quality supervision. If they rate this a 4 or 5, you can bet they are not thrilled with their current situation.

Size of Company: Some people hate bureaucracy and equate the size of a company with the amount of bureaucracy that must be tolerated. Some people prefer small companies because they regard small companies as a better place to learn about their profession and about business in general. On the other hand, some people like the implied security and opportunities offered by a larger company.

Commute: Everybody has thoughts about commuting. Most people want something as close to home as possible. However, there are quite a few who don't consider commuting much of an issue, and there are even some people who say they love a long commute because it gives them an opportunity to kick back, relax and listen to the radio for a couple of hours.

Employee Benefits: This is a complicated issue. Single individuals and people covered by the benefits offered through their spouse's employment aren't as concerned about benefits as most others. I once had a candidate move to another position because his wife needed orthodontic work that was not covered by his current employer. Nowadays any retirement plan that offers early vestment is quite attractive, and so are 401k and other plans that offer tax breaks.

Annual Compensation: This item was intentionally placed at the bottom of the list. The candidate should rank this item three or lower on the *potential employer* side of the ledger.

When compensation is a major issue, you are going to run into problems. You are not in the business of getting a candidate a raise, and the candidate needs to be advised of this in no uncertain terms. If money is a problem, the candidate should approach an immediate supervisor and address the issue with that person. Trying to help a candidate find a better salary is fraught with danger. If you are able to get the candidate a better financial offer from one of your clients, the candidate will probably use it to blackmail the present company into matching the offer. You could lose the placement along with the confidence of your client.

Location(s): Record the locations where the candidate is willing to commute in the space provided.

Annual Compensation: Record the candidate's current compensation here. Include bonuses and money from profit sharing plans. All entries in this area must be dated. It's quite frustrating to get halfway through a placement process only to find that your information about compensation is two years old and the candidate has had two raises since then.

Other Priorities: Of course, there are other possible priorities for each candidate. You need to find out from each candidate what other issues are personally important. For some people, working hours are important because they must drop a child off at school or be home in time to prepare dinner. For others, flex hours may be important in order to avoid intolerable commute traffic. Each candidate will have one or two other issues that, if not discovered at this time, are going to prevent a placement down the line. Be inquisitive!

Times Available for Interviews: Now that you

have taken the time to set up agreements with a candidate, you need to be sure the candidate understands the commitments made to you. Basically the candidate needs to understand that when situations arise that address the expressed concerns, he or she must be willing to explore any opportunities you uncover. This is not a commitment to change jobs. Call it interviewing or call it exploring another position, your candidates must provide times when they are willing to consider other opportunities.

Now you can fill in the reason for leaving at the top of the form. Then we can move to the next chapter where we'll learn how to interview a potential candidate.

CHAPTER 7

THE INTERVIEW

IF YOU'VE GOT
A SOLID FOUNDATION
TO BUILD ON, THE ODDS
ARE DRAMATICALLY
INCREASED THAT
YOU'RE GOING TO
REACH YOUR GOAL.

A well conducted interview ties every aspect of the recruiting business into one tidy package. Interviews are a great source of search assignments and new candidates. Everyone you interview will have information about other potential candidates and other possible search assignments. Part of your job as a recruiter is to tap this resource.

With a few notable exceptions, the interview process is the same for all candidates. One exception occurs when you find yourself talking with an unplaceable person; that is, you discover that the person does not have the professional qualifications you've established for your candidate database. Interviews are very time-consuming, and you cannot afford to interview people outside your area of expertise. Inevitably, you will invite someone in for an interview who turns out to be a poor candidate. This occurs because you are frequently forced to extend an invitation based upon a resumé or a brief phone conversation. Don't feel guilty when you cannot help someone you unwittingly invited to talk with you. People will often lie about their background in order to get you to meet with them, believing that if they can just get in to talk with you, you'll somehow be able to find employment for them.

To the contrary, it would be improper for you to prolong a useless interview and leave someone with the false hope that you will be able to help. As soon as you discover someone is not placeable, let that person know. I generally apologize and emphasize that I specialize in only one area. I say something like, "I'm sorry, but I'm afraid I'm just wasting your valuable time. I'd just be misleading you if I told you I could help with your job search. As I told you over the phone, I only have contacts in the IBM AS400 world. Outside of that specialized area, I probably have fewer contacts than you do."

At this point I stand up and extend my hand. "Thank you very much for coming in. If I should hear of anything in your area I'll let you know, but please don't count on it since I have no contacts in your area of expertise."

If I know of a recruiter who specializes in this person's profession, I will provide that recruiter's name and number. I'll also suggest that the job seeker make sure there is a match before going to see the other recruiter.

The other exception to the standard interview process is with a candidate you've just recruited. Here, you'll omit a few things for reasons that will be made obvious. Before getting on with the interview, examine the forms on the next few pages.

The first form should be filled out by the candidate. You'll fill out the other pages as the interview progresses. Begin as soon as the candidate has completed that first page. The interview should be structured so that the two of you face each other across a small table or desk. You need a surface to write on, situated so that the candidate will have difficulty seeing what you are writing.

First, review the information provided by the candidate on the first page of the interview sheet. This serves several purposes:

» It provides you with a place to start the interview that is non-threatening to the candidate.

» It gives you a chance to make sure everything on the page is legible and accurate before the candidate leaves.

» It gives you an opportunity to make sure everything is filled out completely.

If something is left blank, ask why. For instance, a candidate may omit a work number because calling there would be ill-advised. By discovering this, you can work out other arrangements for getting vital information to the candidate in a timely fashion during regular working hours.

The Work History

On the second page of the interview form, detail the individual's work history. If accounting candidate Jane Roe tells you that all the information you seek is in the resumé, assure her that you have an obligation to learn as much about her work experience as possible to avoid setting up inappropriate interviews. Remember all the questions we asked the hiring manager when taking a search assignment? We need to match all those requirements with the candidate's skills.

COVER SHEET

(To be filled out by Candidate)

YOUR COMPANY NAME

Last name _____ First _____

Street Address

City_____State _____ Zip_____

Mailing Address

City_____State _____ Zip_____

Home phone_____

Work phone _____

Education

Degree	Major	GPA	School	Dates

All other pages to be filled out by recruiter

WORK EXPERIENCE

Current Company _____

Title _____ Supervisor_____ Date Started _____

Duties _____

RFL _____

Salary: Start _____ End _____

Notes _____

_____

Previous Company _____

Title_____ Supervisor _____ Date Started_____

Duties _____

RFL_____

Salary: Start _____ End _____

Notes _____

_____

Previous Company _____

Title _____ Supervisor _____ Date Started _____

Duties _____

RFL_____ _____

Salary: Start _____ End _____

Notes _____

_____

ORGANIZATIONAL CHART FOR XYZ COMPANY

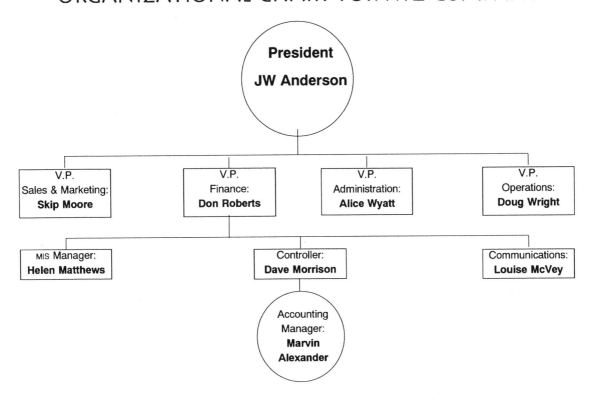

ORGANIZATIONAL CHART OF ACCOUNTING DEPARTMENT

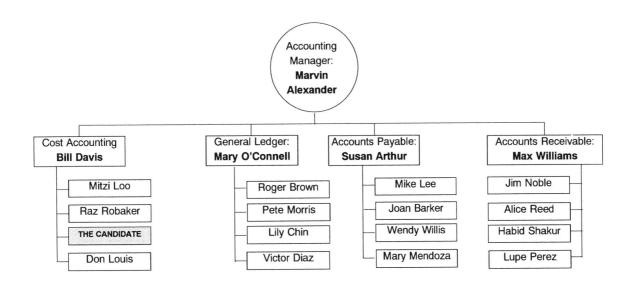

ORGANIZATIONAL CHART FOR_____

Company Structure _____

_____

Total Employees_____

Departmental Structure _____

_____

Total Employees_____

References

Name	Company	Peer/Supervisor	Phone Number

Interviews

Company	Position Description	Interviewed With

Other Agencies

Company	Location	Recruiter

Let's interview Jane Roe. First, you'll need to determine her current title and what it was when she joined the company. Ask her if she has had the same supervisor during her entire stay with the company.

» Ask what her responsibilities were when she first accepted the position and what they are now.

» You also need to know if she is a member of a team and what her role is within that team.

» Does she work with people outside her immediate team?

» Does she work with people outside her department?

» What kind of verbal reports is she required to give and how often?

» What kind of written reports is she required to give and how often?

» Try to learn how much her responsibilities have grown during her tenure in this position. If she appears to have stagnated, try to find out why.

» Find out how much her annual salary was when she first started with her company and how much it is now.

As you begin to ask these questions and discover more and more about Jane's skills and responsibilities, she will become impressed with your depth of knowledge and your obvious interest in her. Actually, the only knowledge you have expressed is your skill in asking the right questions. However, in her eyes you'll have become an intelligent, concerned person. The entire picture of Jane's work experience won't be complete until you've a diagram (or organizational chart) of how she fits into the entire scheme of her company. At this point, hand her a standard $8\frac{1}{2}$ by 11 piece of paper and help her to design an organizational chart showing the staffing arrangement of the company, starting with the head of her department.

Explain to her that you need to understand how her department fits into the hierarchy of the company and how she fits within that hierarchy. Draw a very small circle about three-quarters of the way down the page and label the circle with the name and title of the head of her department. Then ask her who that person reports to. Draw a small circle above the department head and draw a line between the two. Label the new circle with the name and title of the person the department head reports to. Continue this procedure until you have identified the line of command between the head of her department and the president or CEO of the company. If she is cooperative, you can get the names of all the other department heads that report to the same manager, as I've done on page 95, where you'll find a typical company organizational chart that you can use as a project guide.

Once you have an overview of how the company is structured, you need to determine how Jane fits into the structure of her department. Once again, start with an $8\frac{1}{2}$ by 11 sheet of paper, only this time the head of the department will appear as a small circle at the top center of the paper. Once again the circle should be labeled with the manager's name and title. The bottom half of page 95 is a diagram of the structure of a medium size accounting department. Use it as an example, if your candidate needs help. Determine who reports directly to the department manager, including names and titles. Generally this will include one or more supervisors responsible for certain projects. Once the supervisors are in place, you can identify who Jane reports to and exactly where her position is within the department. Next you need to determine who her peers are within her particular group and what role each plays in the projects the group is responsible for. This process is rather delicate and needs to proceed slowly and deliberately.

"Now that we have determined what projects your group is responsible for, I need to see how you fit within this picture. What are your major responsibilities within these projects?"

Ask Jane to point to the chart and name the person with whom she interfaces most frequently.

"What other people do you interface with fairly frequently and what part of the project do they work on?" Again, these people need to be labeled and named on the chart.

"Does your department do any cross training so that you can fill in for someone while on vacation? Who are you cross trained to fill in for?" Label and name these people.

Once you have determined the names and responsibilities of the people in Jane's group, it's time to move on to the other groups within the department. Ask, "Do you ever work with people in any other group? If so, which ones?"

If your candidate wants to know why this is important, make sure she understands that the more exposure she has to other functions in the department, the more valuable she is going to be in the marketplace. This will impact the type and number of jobs she will be qualified to handle and the salary level she can command.

Finally, go back to the company organizational chart the two of you put together earlier. Find out who Jane interfaced with outside her department. Have her identify them, including their responsibilities and the nature of her interaction with each of them.

By the time you've finished this exercise, you'll have a complete picture of exactly what Jane has done in her current position, what she's been exposed to, who she's worked with and what training she's received. You are now in a position to represent her with complete authority, and to match her skills against any search assignment you might have now or in the future.

By taking the time to explore the capabilities of this candidate so thoroughly, you've also won her loyalty and her confidence. No one is now better qualified to represent her interests than you are, with the possible exception of Jane herself. Your reward for taking this time is manifold. You are in a better position than anyone else to find her an appropriate position and, thus, the most likely to please a client and receive the commensurate placement fee. Moreover, you now have the names of a sizable list of people who you know are the types of professionals you can use in your database. Depending on the size of the department the candidate is working in, you may have picked up as many as ten new names. You also have the names of two or more potential hiring managers, the department head and the supervisor(s). You also know that there is a vacancy in the department (if Jane's already left) or that there soon will be.

A carefully considered examination of a

candidate's background can bring you both great rewards.

You can now understand why it's important to be sure the candidate you are interviewing is a placeable candidate; that is, a candidate who conforms to your professional profile. You've just spent a lot of time—yours and your candidate's. Make sure it is time well spent. You have the names of several potential recruits and hiring managers. If you've interviewed the wrong candidate, these names are worthless.

Page 94 contains a form that will allow you to record information on the candidate's current (or recently vacated) position, and on two previous positions. As a general rule, it is unnecessary to talk in any depth about positions the candidate has held prior to the most current three. In addition, it is usually unnecessary to explore a candidate's work record beyond the past six years. I call this my 3/6 rule. Any work experience the candidate had prior to the last three positions or over six years ago is probably not relevant to a current search. The only time I break the 3/6 rule and look for information beyond what is offered on the resumé is if the candidate has had more than three positions in the last six years or if the candidate has been in the same position or department for over six years.

If the candidate has been changing positions rather quickly you need to know why. Most clients are suspicious of candidates who change positions frequently. However, sometimes such moves are unavoidable and you need to know that. The best designed plans of a candidate can be thwarted by unexpected layoffs or company closure or relocation. Unavoidable job changes can sometimes be used to advantage; for example, in demonstrating to

a hiring manager the importance to a candidate of finding a permanent home where the candidate can stay for a long time. "After having two companies go bad on him, my candidate is really sensitive about finding a place where he can grow for a good many years." That's music to a hiring manager's ears.

If a candidate has been with the same company for over six years, the candidate's career path needs to be well-documented. Someone who's stayed in the same position for over six years is not going to appear very attractive. However, if you can demonstrate that the person has moved up the ladder in terms of technical achievement or assumed responsibility, the problem will vanish and the candidate can become quite attractive because of the long term commitment to one company.

Reason For Leaving

Check the agreement form that we discussed last chapter. If the candidate has already quit, or is about to do so, there'll be no doubt about the "Reason For Leaving" (RFL). In this case, you need do nothing more than enter that information at the top of the agreement form. However, if this is a recently recruited candidate, you'll need to follow the procedures described in Chapter 6 for establishing an RFL. The only two agreements you must establish with a candidate determined to leave a current position is salary and interview times.

Regardless of whether you're dealing with a recruited candidate or one who is ready to leave his or her current position, one rule is always the same. Beware of the candidate who is leaving because of inadequate compensation. You are not in the business of getting people raises. If that is the only concern, your candidate should address that issue with his or her boss, not with you. You certainly have no desire to tell an inquiring hiring manager that your candidate is looking for a new position because of money. After all, even an inexperienced hiring manager will know that there are other professionals working in the same company who are not upset by the salary structure. You and your candidate would be looked upon with suspicion.

Be sure you really understand the RFL; make sure it is realistic. This is important. Everyone wants to know why a candidate is leaving (or has left) a current position. You are going to have to explain this to the hiring manager, and you need to feel comfortable with the reason. It should be something that can be verified. When representing the candidate to a hiring manager, it is much more effective to let a reference or two speak on the candidate's behalf.

"My candidate is looking for a new position because the company is in very bad shape financially and he is afraid of being caught in a downsizing effort. I verified this with several other people who are familiar with the current status of this company's finances. A lot of other employees are equally concerned."

Another important reason to make sure the RFL is legitimate is that you'll want to use it as a tool to recruit other professionals from the same company. If some situation is having enough of an impact to make your candidate seriously consider leaving a current position, the same thing must also be impacting coworkers. You'll want to capitalize on this when you recruit your candidate's peers. Next chapter, we'll discuss recruiting your candidate's

references, and we'll deal with this issue in more depth.

Some RFLs are recognized as legitimate and can be accepted without verification. The following list is by no means complete. There are many other legitimate reasons why a candidate might consider leaving a company or position.

» "The company has brought in an outside manager for our department. I and many of my associates are having trouble with his very authoritarian style."

» "I didn't mind commuting for an hour, but now the traffic is so bad my commute is up to an hour and a half."

» "The company is going through some major financial problems. We've already had two layoffs. I'm afraid I'll be next."

» "I've held the same position for almost three years and have learned everything it has to offer. In talking to my manager, it appears there aren't going to be any opportunities for personal growth in the foreseeable future. It is obvious that I need to look outside the company for any career growth."

» "When I took the position I was unaware that one of the company's major clients was the U.S. Army. I do not believe in supporting a military organization." (Since this is a moral issue, a potential hiring manager needs to know about the candidate's stand. After all, the hiring manager could be a proud member of the army reserves.)

» "Our company has become very bureaucratic as a result of growth. I do not thrive in that kind of environment."

» "Our company still uses the 123 system and has no plans to upgrade. I'm afraid that if I stay here much longer my technical skills will become too antiquated to interest another company."

» "Our company plans to move its headquarters out of the area. I'm not in a position to move with the company."

Other RFLs should only be accepted after they have been verified:

» "I can't get along with the people in my office." Candidates who complain about a fellow worker or manager may themselves be difficult to get along with. Verify the situation before trying to explain this to a potential hiring manager.

» "My supervisor is a tyrant!" Hiring managers won't want to hire a chronic complainer.

» "They want me to work past five." In many professions, putting in overtime is considered normal.

References

On page 96, just below the company and department organizational notes, you'll see a section for references. Although there are only spaces for five references, you should get as many as possible.

If the candidate has work experience prior to the current position, you'll already have the names of previous managers. Find out if the candidate has maintained contact with these managers. If not, ask for help in tracking them down.

Get references from peers who have knowledge of the candidate's previous positions. Peers tend to give more favorable references than managers. Regardless of why the candidate left a position, the manager may harbor resentment because the candidate abandoned ship, possibly at a time the manager considered critical. The manager may also feel obliged to give a completely unbiased assessment of the candidate's capabilities, which means pointing out small flaws. Peers, on the other hand, are more likely to give warm and fuzzy references. The candidate and the peer were friends who probably admired each other's work and may have faced a common foe together, possibly that very manager.

If your candidate is reluctant to help you locate these references, mention that the option could be more unpleasant. If you can't find references from past positions, more references will be required from current co-workers. Most candidates don't want too many people where they are currently working to know that they are actively seeking other employment.

Should the candidate (let's call this one Tom) question why references are needed now, offer the following examples of possible conversations with a hiring manager:

Without References

"I have a candidate I think will fit very well in the position you currently have open. I have interviewed Tom and believe that he has all the skills you are looking for."

With References

"I have a candidate I know will do very well in the position you currently have open. I have talked to five people Tom has worked with and they all agree that he is an excellent candidate. Not only have they verified that Tom has all the skills you are looking for, but each person volunteered that he is a hard worker who gets along exceptionally well with everyone. When I described your position to them, they were unanimous in their opinion that Tom would be perfect for the position."

Then ask Tom which scenario would play best with the hiring manager.

In addition to the references you have already acquired from a candidate's previous positions, you will need some references from his or her current position. If the candidate has already left that position, you want to be the one who determines the best references. For this purpose, go back to the departmental organizational chart you put together with the candidate. Pick out co-workers you think will make good references and good recruits. Tell the candidate you wish to talk with these people about his or her background and experiences.

Don't let the candidate pick the references. If you're asked why, explain that the references you pick out are going to carry a lot more weight than the prescreened references a candidate selects. Random references are unbiased, and this will have a much greater impact on the hiring manager.

If the candidate is still working, the selection process must be different because of the possibility that the news will get around that he or she is looking for a new position. In all likelihood, the candidate has confided in one or more co-workers. Find out who these confidantes are and promise to make the queries at home after work. This is almost always satisfactory to the candidate.

If you are working with a recruited candidate, on the other hand, not even the candidate knows that a new job may be in the offing.

Therefore, you must guarantee the candidate's security. Don't discuss the eventual need for references until all the agreements between you and the candidate are in place. Mutually select the references that the candidate knows can maintain confidentiality. As part of your agreement with the recruited candidate, promise that none of these people will be contacted until after the candidate has found a new position and an offer awaits only the reference checks.

Interviews

Since they have not been actively looking for new positions, recruited candidates have not gone out on interviews, but candidates who are actively looking for another position may have already been interviewed by some companies, and this should concern you. If you are not diligent in determining what companies the candidate has contacted, both you and the candidate can run into problems. Candidates may be reluctant to give out this information for fear you might immediately send out thirty competitors to interview for the same position. Therefore, it is important that they understand why you need this information.

First, you want to avoid accidentally representing Jane to a client who has already interviewed her. This creates a conflict in the eyes of the client, and Jane is usually automatically eliminated as a contender for the position. This is a standard practice that most companies employ to prevent an unscrupulous recruiter from trying to collect an undeserved fee. The practice can hurt your relationship with the client as well. You are going to seem incompetent for not being aware that Jane had already contacted them.

You also need to review, in detail, the positions where Jane has interviewed to find out what type of positions she has considered, and what she liked and disliked about those positions. By reviewing each position in detail, you are less apt to embarrass yourself or Jane by setting up an interview for an unacceptable position or with an inappropriate company.

Assure Jane that you will not contact any company or hiring manager where she maintains a strong interest in a position. However, where she has little interest in a position, there should be no reluctance to provide you with as much information as possible. After all, you are going to be spending a lot of your valuable time marketing her talents to your clients. In turn, you should have access to information about positions she has no interest in.

Other Agencies

It is common practice among recruiters to try to find out about any other recruiters a candidate might also be working with. There is a legitimate reason for this. Clients won't consider a candidate represented by more than one recruiter. To protect yourself and your candidate, you need to know where other recruiters are sending Jane.

Unscrupulous recruiters, however, may use candidates to find out about search assignments other recruiters are working on. Knowing this, most recruiters will delay telling a candidate the name of the company where they are going to interview until the last minute, and they then make the candidate swear not to divulge any information about positions the recruiter has told him or her about.

This might place Candidate Tony in an awkward position. If he doesn't divulge the in-

formation, he risks being represented to a company by two different recruiters. On the other hand, if he reveals the information, he could incur a recruiter's wrath.

Some candidates assume that the more recruiters they contact, the more exposure they will get. I try to make Tony understand that this only creates problems and doesn't guarantee him anything. In fact, it could actually limit his exposure. I explain that, as a specialist, I work only in his area of expertise. I am therefore acutely aware of just about everything that goes on in this limited marketplace. He will miss very little by limiting his activities to a single recruiter. I further advise Tony that he needs to maintain complete control over who represents him, and when and where he is represented. I suggest that he contact the other recruiters and notify them that he no longer wishes to be represented by them. Candidates willing to do this elicit much more enthusiasm from me, and I tell them so.

Another method I use to protect myself from recruiters eager to find out about my search assignments from shared candidates requires the cooperation of hiring managers. Obviously, having an exclusive helps keep other recruiters away. Getting four or six candidates before the hiring manager also helps immeasurably. However, there is always the chance that one or two persuasive recruiters will find their way in the door. Therefore, I advise the hiring manager ahead of time that word will eventually get out that a position is open and that other recruiters will prove pestiferous. To save time and exasperation, I suggest that the hiring manager refer those recruiters to me. I will be more than happy to sort through the candidates offered by other recruiters so the mandates offered by other recruiters so the manager doesn't have to deal with all the resumés and phone calls. That way I can be sure the manager gets to select from the six best candidates, and I still have complete control over the hiring process. The very worst that can happen is I might have to split the fee with another recruiter.

INTERVIEWING TABOOS

A multitude of laws govern the employment process, so it is best to be aware of what you can and cannot ask a candidate during an interview. Since, as a recruiter, you only screen candidates and don't make hiring decisions, there is some question as to whether the laws apply to you. However, it is best to be aware of them.

You cannot ask:

» "Where were you born?"

» "Where were your parents born?"

» "What is your (or a relative's) citizenship?"

» "How did you learn to read, write or speak a foreign language?"

» "Have you had any foreign military service?"

» ...or any other question relating to nationality.

You can ask:

» "If hired, can you submit verification of your legal right to work in the United States?" (Citizenship verification may be questioned if the position requires it, as in a security clearance.)

You cannot ask:

» "What is your birth date?"

» "How old are you?"

» "What date did you complete high school or elementary school?"

You can ask:

» "Can you submit a birth certificate or other proof of age if you are hired?"

» "Are you over 18 years of age?"

» "Can you submit a work permit after hiring, if you are under 18 years of age?"

You cannot ask:

» "Do you own your own home or do you rent?"

» "What is your marital status?"

» "What is the number and/or age of your dependents?"

» "With whom do you reside?"

You can ask:

» "Where do you reside?"

» "Are you available to work evenings and weekends?" (If the position would require such a schedule.)

You cannot ask:

» "What is your maiden name?"

You can ask:

» "Have you ever used a different name?"

You cannot ask:

» "What is your general state of health?"

» "What is your height?"

» "What is your weight?"

» ...or any questions about childbearing, pregnancy, birth control, or family responsibilities.

You can ask:

» "Do you have any medical history that would limit your ability to perform the job applied for, or to perform the job without endangering the health or safety of yourself or others?"

You cannot ask:

» "Are you handicapped?"

» "Do you have any disabilities?"

You can ask:

» "Do you have any physical condition or handicap that may limit your ability to perform the job you are applying for? If so, what can be done to accommodate the limitation?"

You cannot ask:

» "What is the name and address of a relative to be notified in case of emergency?"

You can ask:

» "What is the name and address of the person to be notified in case of emergency?"

You cannot ask:

» "Have you ever been arrested?"

You can ask:

» "Have you ever been convicted of a crime?"

(This inquiry should only be made if the job requirements are such that relevant convictions would clearly be disqualifiers. Such query should be accompanied by a statement that the existence of a criminal record does not constitute an automatic bar to employment.)

You cannot ask:

» "Are you now receiving, or have you ever received workers' compensation benefits?"

» "Have you ever filed a workers' compensation claim?"

You can ask:

» "Give the names of persons willing to provide professional and/or character references."

You cannot ask:

» "What is your religion?"

» "What religious holidays do you observe?"

» "What is your sex?"

» "What is your complexion?"

» "What is your race?"

» "What is your eye or hair color?"

» ...or any questions pertaining to an applicant's current or past assets, liabilities, or credit rating, including bankruptcy or garnishment.

Actually, as recruiters, we never ask for this information anyway. The information we need is in the next chapter, so let's find out how to check references.

CHAPTER 8

REFERENCE CHECKS

YOU CANNOT
TAILOR-MAKE THE
SITUATIONS IN LIFE, BUT
YOU CAN TAILOR-MAKE
THE ATTITUDES TO FIT
THOSE SITUATIONS.

Workers Make Bosses Pay For Bad References, the headline blared in the San Francisco Examiner (August 2, 1987) According to the article, former employees of companies all across the nation were suing past employers for giving out bad references. The average award was $428,000 for each suit filed, and there were a lot of them. Jury Verdict Research Inc. reported that one-third of all slander and libel verdicts for the previous five years targeted employers. No one can say for sure what the figure is today, but almost all companies soon stopped giving out references on employees. It was just too risky.

Anyone calling for a reference nowadays is directed to personnel, which will only confirm the dates that the employee worked for the company, the employee's job titles, work locations and, perhaps, salary. Most companies won't give out good or bad references, and managers are warned neither to criticize nor praise former employees. Legal advisers fear that once a company begins giving out good references, a failure to give out any reference might be seen as negative. No one wants to risk a possible law suit.

This has created a real dilemma for hiring managers and candidates alike. Hiring managers find it frustrating, since they have always relied on references to select the right employees. Things are not much better for candidates, who have depended upon praise to help them find work. The only people who gain from this reference paranoia are candidates with bad work records. When I researched the backgrounds of some candidates, I discovered that a number of them had reference "plants," usually friends who were willing to lie about them. One plant swore that a candidate worked for a particular company for over a year. Luckily, I decided to dig more deeply after discovering a slight discrepancy in the dates of employment. It turned out that the company had never heard of the candidate who had supposedly work for them for fifteen months. I also knew of an MIS manager who was fired from four different positions in less than a year and no one was the wiser. Since the hiring companies couldn't get information from former employers, they relied on the candidates planted references in making their hiring decision. These documented incidents of undesirable employees taking advantage of reference paranoia represent the tip of the iceberg.

The only people who can avoid this problem are recruiters, because they can get references without being afraid that they themselves or the referring company will get sued. Used properly, the recruiter's ability to obtain legitimate reference checks can be a powerful selling tool. Every hiring manager will feel much more comfortable selecting a candidate who has good references than selecting a candidate whose references are inaccessible or, worse, planted. You just need to let the manager know that you will be able to provide candidates whose references have been or can be thoroughly examined. No manager likes to make a hiring mistake, regardless of the circumstances. They feel it reflects badly on their ability as managers. You can help them avoid making that mistake.

THE PROFILE

Since companies are no longer willing to give references, how can recruiters get this information? The answer is really very simple. A recruiter has a right to know all about a candidate before deciding whether or not to represent that person. In essence, the recruiter is not doing reference checks to determine if someone should or should not be hired but to develop a profile of a potential candidate to determine how and if to represent that person.

This may seem like a fine line, but it isn't. As a recruiter, I have the right to protect my business and my reputation. Most clients depend on recruiters to present them with candidates who have been thoroughly screened. They have a right to demand accurate information. So, although recruiters do not make hiring decisions, the information they provide will influence hiring decisions.

A recruiter can develop a candidate profile without risking a lawsuit, because the profile is an assemblage of information from a number of sources. Specific information cannot be traced to a single individual or company.

Therefore, the candidate has no one to sue if the overall profile is less than complimentary. Since the recruiter does not release information but merely compiles it, the recruiter is immune from legal action. The recruiter merely decides whether or not to represent the candidate to his clients. If the recruiter decides not to represent the candidate, the profile is never seen by any hiring authority. At the same time, the recruiter in no way infringes on the right of candidates to represent themselves to any company.

When you gather information about a candidate, be sure to let the person providing the reference (henceforth referred to as "the evaluator") know exactly what you are doing. Once it's understood that a lawsuit cannot result, individuals and companies are usually more than happy to discuss the candidates. I straight-away tell the evaluator I am not doing reference checks. I say something like, "I have been asked to represent the candidate in a job search and I am putting together a profile. Whatever you tell me cannot be traced back to you. My goal is to put together an honest evaluation, so

I can represent the candidate truthfully or, should the information warrant it, decline representation."

No one has ever turned me down. However, I have had one or two people ask that I call them at home. They did not feel comfortable talking with me from work because of the restrictions placed on them by the company. Nor have I run across a candidate or hiring manager opposed to the concept of the profile. Hiring managers consider the profile an essential tool in their hiring decisions. Candidates, except maybe those with poor work records, see it as a means of getting a vote of confidence from their peers and former managers.

Here are two actual examples of candidate profiles, one put together by an associate and one by me. Only the names have been changed.

The letter on page 110 was submitted after the company had decided to make an offer of employment to John, pending good references. On pages 111–112 is a profile I submitted before a company decided whom to hire.

To: Hiring Manager
        LMNOP Co.
From: J. J. Recruiter
        Consultant

I have completed a profile of John Doe's background and experiences. Most comments were favorable, indicating that John was a dedicated, loyal employee who worked diligently in a very confused, poorly managed situation. All references commented on John's personality, his great "user interface abilities," "people-oriented attitude," "a person who is extremely easy to get along with." Additionally, they all commented on John as a "technically good... great analyst," who was good in obtaining details as well as general concepts, provided very good programming ("a sharp programmer") and excellent documentation. John appears to know and understand the need to obtain help, guidance or whatever is necessary to complete the task on time. He provides feedback whether good or bad. All commend John for his knowledge of manufacturing systems, from design to implementation, but also comment on his support and work with the accounting areas. His verbal communication abilities can be enhanced, but never failed to define what was required.

Finally, while John did not prosper in the XYZ situation, most all references believe that John will do very well at LMNOP Co. The positive and supportive management at LMNOP enthuses John and will no doubt make the difference in his success. I look forward to talking to both you and John in the near future, and of your success in bring LMNOP's new data processing program into being. It was indeed a pleasure working with such a professional, decision making company.

Respectfully submitted,

J.J. Recruiter

To: Hiring Manager
        QRST Co.
From: Richard Mackie
        Consultant

I have completed references for Jane Doe. Comments concerning Jane border on the extraordinary, and it was obvious that she is greatly admired. All three references worked closely with Jane, depended upon her heavily at times, and were never disappointed. All commented that she is a very "goal oriented" individual who is "conscientious," "industrious" and "well organized."

They were unanimous in their opinion that one of her greatest strengths lies in her ability to communicate effectively with individuals at all levels from senior executive to the assembly line worker. Her ability to take very complex issues, break them down into appropriate components, then explain them in a fashion that even the most uninformed could grasp, is a key to her communication skills. Her natural aptitude for conveying complex information to others while making them feel competent and involved, has made her relationships with those she works strong and supportive. Two of those interviewed commented that Jane is very social and that many of her professional relationships evolved into very open and comfortable friendships.

Her two associates at PPR felt that she accomplished a small miracle by rebuilding the entire service department in the short period of two months while maintaining an acceptable level of service to the clients and reducing the backlog of calls from 600 to thirty. Her manager at UUW commented that Jane developed all their educational materials and that they were so well done that they are still used today virtually unchanged.

Persistent efforts by me to illicit some comments regarding possible weaknesses or areas where Jane might improve yielded very little. One finally suggested that Jane might occasionally be too tenacious. Not in the stubborn way, but in taking a task and going with it. In her fervor to get a project done well and on time she will occasionally leave others behind.

I described the position with your company for which Jane has applied and received the following comments:

"The position would fit Jane's personality and background perfectly."

"I can't think of anyone who could do it better. She would bring a whole new level of commitment and expertise to the position."

"It sounds like a perfect fit."

All three people are willing to serve as official references. Listed below are the names and phone numbers of the individuals with whom I spoke. They would all be happy to speak with you further about any aspect of Jane's performance and expertise.

Respectfully Submitted,

Richard A. Mackie
Consultant

This profile served its purpose. The company decided to hire my candidate. She served in the position very well for over three years. After three years, her assignment was done and both she and the company recognized that it was time for her to move on. However, the company was so pleased with what she had accomplished, they asked me to find her replacement.

GATHERING THE INFORMATION

At the same time that you gather reference information from a peer or a manager, you'll be developing a relationship with that person. Your hope is that the relationship will lead to a good recruit or a good search assignment.

Look at the forms that appear on pages 114–115 and 116–117. The first is used for getting information from a peer and the second for getting information from a manager. When you duplicate these forms, allow plenty of room to record the answers provided by the evaluator.

Make sure you have filled in the information in the box at the top of the first page of the form before making the call. I generally start the conversation with a candidate's peer or a manager in this way:

"Good evening. My name is Richard Mackie. Jane Doe has asked me to represent her in a job search and she has given me your name as someone who can fill me in on her background and experience. Is this a good time or should I call back when it is more convenient?"

Most people don't want to mess up Jane's chances of finding a job, so they always cooperate, even if I have to call back later. Once they are ready for me to start, I ask the first question without any additional chit chat. I want them to regard me as a professional first and a friend later.

Peer Evaluation

1. Make sure that everyone concerned—you, the candidate, and the evaluator—understand the nature of the relationship between the candidate and the evaluator. You need to understand where the reference is "coming from" when your questions are answered. An evaluator with more experience may have greater expectations of your candidate than someone with much less experience. Usually, a less experienced evaluator will tend to "look up" to your more experienced candidate. Those with more experience may tend to "look down" on your candidate.

2. Obviously, you are interested in determining whether your candidate worked independently or as part of a team.

3. If the candidate was part of a team, confirm the various projects your candidate claimed as the team's responsibility. (You might use the term "accomplishment" instead of "responsibility." However, the evaluator is likely to address only completed projects if you ask about accomplishments. Obviously, it is best to ask about both.) If the candidate worked independently, confirm that he or she worked on the projects claimed.

4. If your candidate was part of a team, determine how the projects were distributed.

5. is self-explanatory, and so are 6 and 7.

Professional Profile: Peer Reference

Candidate Name _____ Date _____

Evaluator's Name _____ Phone_____

Evaluator's Company _____ Phone_____

Evaluator's Title _____ Recruiter_____

1. What was your working relationship with_____? _____

   _____

2. Was he/she part of a group_____ How many in group? _____

3. What were group's responsibilities (accomplishments)?_____

   _____

4. How was work distributed? _____

5. What tasks (assignments) did_____have sole responsibility for? _____

   _____

6. Was_____considered a (junior, senior) member of group? _____

7. Did_____finish tasks in a timely fashion? _____

8. Which of _____ professional attributes impressed you most? _____

   _____

9. Which of _____ personal attributes impressed you most?_____

   _____

10. Which professional attributes could be strengthened? _____

11. Which personal attributes could be strengthened? _____

12. How was_____relationship with others? _____

    Peers? _____ Supervisors? _____ Subordinates? _____

    Others? _____

13. What adjectives would you use to describe_____? _____

    _____

Other comments _____

Reason For Leaving

1._____ tells me he/she is (looking, leaving, left) because _____

_____

Is this your understanding?_____

_____

2. Is this situation impacting others in company? _____

3. Is this situation impacting others in group?_____

4. Is this situation impacting you? _____ In what way? _____

_____

Perhaps we need to get together to discuss some options for you.

When can we get together? Date _____ Time _____

5. Not recruitable because_____

_____

6. Not placeable because _____

_____

Notes

Professional Profile: Manager Reference

Candidate Name _____ Date _____

Evaluator's Name _____ Phone _____

Evaluator's Company _____ Phone _____

Evaluator's Title _____ Recruiter _____

1. What was your working relationship with_____? _____

_____

2. Was _____part of a group? _____ How many in group? _____

3. What were the group's responsibilities (accomplishments)? _____

_____

4. How was work distributed? _____

5. What tasks (assignments) did_____ have sole responsibility for?_____

_____

6. Was he/she considered a (junior, senior) member of group? _____

7. Did he/she finish tasks in a timely fashion? _____

8. How much supervision did he/she require? _____

*9. Does he/she work well independently and in a group? _____

*10. Is he/she cooperative?_____ Goal oriented?_____

*11. How are his/her oral skills? _____ Written skills? _____

*12. Which of his/her professional attributes impressed you most?_____

*13. Which of his/her personal attributes impressed you most? _____

*14. Which professional attributes could be strengthened? _____

*15. Which personal attributes could be strengthened? _____

*16. Did_____ have good interpersonal relationships with his/her peers? _____

    supervisors? _____ subordinates? _____

    others in the company? _____others outside the company? _____

17. Which relationships were most important in his/her position? _____

18. What adjectives would you use to describe him/her? _____

_____

19. Is he/she eligible for rehire should an appropriate position open at a later date?_____

* Are these important (skills, attributes) you look for when hiring?

Search Assignment

1. You mentioned on several occasions that you look for employees that are _____

   _____

2. How do you find such people? _____

   _____

3. How do you verify their skills and attributes? _____

   _____

4. Have you ever used a recruiter to fill a position? _____

   Was it a rewarding or bad experience? _____

   _____

5. Do you have any (current, anticipated) openings?_____

   _____

<u>Notes</u>

I'm breezing through the questions here, but you should take your time. Your secondary purpose is to get acquainted with the person giving the reference. Once the evaluator understands that you are a professional (as demonstrated by your professional questions), begin showing your friendly side. A little chit-chat or friendly observations are always in order. When you have finished gathering information from a peer, you'll want that evaluator to become one of your candidates. Candidates want a recruiter who is competent but also someone they can feel comfortable talking with when things aren't going so well at work.

8. This question always elicits an interesting response. If the candidate is more experienced than the evaluator, you will generally hear high praise about your candidate's technical skills. The evaluator may have learned a lot from your candidate. If the situation is reversed, the response may focus on your candidate's ability to learn quickly or grasp concepts, since the evaluator may be the teacher. Sometimes the evaluator needs a little prompting, in which case ask directly about the candidate's technical skills or ability to grasp new concepts, etc.

9. Evaluators often get Question #8 and #9 mixed up. That's all right. Your goal is to illicit positive comments about your candidate. Answers to this question are extremely variable from "gets along well with everybody" to "goes to church every Sunday." Standing alone, such comments may not seem significant. However, you'll be surprised how often three or four different evaluators will comment on the same thing. When you put together the candidate's profile, it looks good to be able to say that all four references contained comments on the candidate's "ability to get along well with everybody."

10. At one time, it was popular to ask the evaluator to identify the candidate's weaknesses. The responses rarely had value because the question was threatening. That's why I ask the same question in a more positive light. By asking what attribute could be strengthened, I get more enlightened responses, usually accompanied by an explanation. "Jane is a little weak in the development of cost systems. However, this is because she did not have much opportunity to deal with them. She was always busy on other projects."

11. Here, too, placing the question in a positive context elicits a much better response. It was by using this technique that I finally got someone to comment on Jane's tendency to be too tenacious at times (in the profile letter discussed earlier this chapter).

Don't pass over the last two questions lightly. They are very important for two reasons:

» You want to avoid any unpleasant surprises that might reflect back on you after you have placed the candidate with one of your clients.

» Nobody is perfect. Your profile of the candidate will carry a lot more weight if it shows that the candidate is "only human." There may be a few flaws, but nothing that would keep the candidate from doing a good job for the company. The hiring manager wants an honest evaluation of the candidate and not a "snow job."

12. You'll need considerably more room to write down the answer to this question. It says a good deal about a person's success in the work place. A simple "good" or "okay" response is not good enough. You need more. Regardless of how wonderful a candidate might otherwise be, be wary of anyone whose ability to develop positive relationships is suspect. People who have difficulty getting along with other people are not usually appreciated by hiring managers. This doesn't mean that a candidate who has had problems with one particular employee should be blacklisted. You are concerned about those few that seemed to have some difficulty dealing with people wherever they go.

13. This is one of my favorite questions because the responses are so spontaneous and honest. I usually say something like, "Now I want you to think about Jane and tell me the first four adjectives that pop into your mind."

The "Other comments" area is to be used as you see fit. In the course of answering other questions, the evaluator will often make comments about the candidate that are not related to the current topic. Record these comments here.

Reason For Leaving

By this time, you and the evaluator should be on pretty friendly terms. In addition to learning about your candidate, you should have learned enough about the person providing the evaluation to determine if he or she is candidate material. If the evaluator is a good potential candidate, here's where you begin turning the call into a recruiting call. The RFL is the key to making this switch.

1. This is a critical question. It's important to verify your candidate's RFL, and in most cases the evaluator will be able to do this. However, there are instances where the candidate has not confided in this particular person, and the evaluator will not be able to provide verification. In such a situation, you may want to discover an RFL for the evaluator. You might ask if there are problems that might influence people to consider leaving. Once the evaluator has confirmed the candidate's RFL or has come up with another RFL, you are ready to proceed.

2. This question, as well as the next two, is designed to get the evaluator to think about the magnitude of the problem, first from a company perspective and then on a personal level. By starting at the company level, the evaluator will not feel alone or guilty about reacting to the situation in a negative manner. You want this potential candidate to feel comfortable about discussing the problem with you on a personal level.

Once the evaluator has vented, invite him or her to get together with you to discuss some options. This is not, however, the time to start mentioning job changes. That would be far too threatening at this point. Your goal is to meet and put together the agreements we talked about in previous chapters.

5. Some people are just not recruitable. If this evaluator is not recruitable, make a note of it so you won't try again at another time.

6. You may discover during the reference check that the evaluator does not have the

skills or talents you are looking for. In this case, make no attempt at recruiting the evaluator. Again, make a note to this effect so you don't attempt to recruit this person at a later date.

The Hiring Manager's Evaluation

As you can see, the first part of the form designed for taking reference information from a hiring manager is identical to that used for gathering information from peers who provide references. The first seven queries also closely match the questions you would ask a hiring manager when taking a search assignment. In all three instances, the questions are not only designed to gather information but to impress the hiring manager. You are not the typical recruiter who says, "Tell me about Tom Adams." You are a unique recruiter who asks probing questions that tells the manager you know what you are doing. By the time you finish these first seven questions, the manager will understand that you know what is important in evaluating an employee.

8. Only the manager is qualified to answer this question.

Questions #9 through #16 are preceded by an asterisk. They are special questions that may lead to a search assignment. Each of these questions will help you learn what the hiring manager looks for in an employee. For instance, after receiving Mary Smith's evaluation of Tom's ability to work independently and in a group, you might ask the following: "I noticed that you seem particularly pleased with this attribute of Tom's. Is this something you look for when you hire someone?" Make a note of her response under #1 on the second page of this form.

If you notice a similar enthusiasm when talking about the issues addressed in Questions #10 and #11, you might investigate further with a question such as, "I couldn't help but get the feeling that this is very important to you. Why is that?" Note the response.

Questions #12 to #15 are identical to questions that are asked in the form used for peer references. Anticipate a totally different response to these questions from the manager. Peers will often comment on a candidate's technical skill or knowledge while a manager almost never does. To the manager, skill and knowledge are a part of the experience level of a candidate. Managers who want someone with a higher level of skill look for a more senior (more experienced) person. Therefore, managers will assume the candidate's skill level is in place and will be more concerned with intangibles.

Generally, you can assume Mary Smith will look for the same qualities in a new employee that Tom impressed her with. Likewise, what she thinks could be strengthened in Tom will be sought after in a new employee. It doesn't hurt to question the manager's responses in more depth. "I noticed that you were quite enthusiastic about Tom's ability to think things through to a proper conclusion. Is this something you try to look for in an employee?" All information gathered from these questions should also be noted near the bottom of your form.

16. Dealing with employees has a lot in common with dealing with kids. Nobody likes disciplinary problems. Hiring managers want employees to get along well together. Therefore, they are very anxious to weed out troublemakers or malcontents. The manager providing you with this reference will be aware of this, and you want Mary to know that you are aware of it, too. Talk about this subject in depth, for your sake, your client's sake and the manager's sake. Nothing will kill your business quicker than placing a troublemaker with a client.

17. Confirm where your candidate spent time. Tom might have said, "I reported to the V.P. of Operations," because it sounds prestigious. The manager will know the precise nature of each assignment.

18. Here, again, is an opportunity to elicit a spontaneous response.

19. This used to be a standard question; however, it was one of the first questions to disappear, because it became a major cause of lawsuits. Obviously, if your old employer doesn't want you back, why should a new employer consider hiring you? We ask this question a little differently, so there's no misunderstanding. We do not want Mary to feel pressured to rehire Tom. The key to this question is the word "eligible." This does not commit her to hiring him; it just assures you that the candidate has not been blacklisted for some reason. When writing a profile, it carries a good deal of weight to be able to declare that "Tom is eligible for rehire everywhere he worked."

Search Assignment

By this time, the manager providing the reference should have a good deal of respect for your professionalism and feel comfortable talking with you. By the same token, you are now aware that what a manager wants to know most about a potential employee cannot be found in a candidate's resumé or through an interview. It can only be found through good reference checks. You also know that managers have little if any access to reference information except through you. Armed with this knowledge, you should have little trouble persuading this manager to look to you when a position becomes available.

» You have already recorded whatever information you garnered about Mary Smith's hiring preferences when asking Questions #9 through #16. You may know, for example, that she looks for a candidate who can work well in a group or independently, is cooperative and goal oriented, and possesses good oral and written skills. Perhaps she places a good deal of importance on employees who can think things through and follow a project to completion. In addition, you may have found out that she must have employees who get along well with peers as well as with other people in the company. Confirm your assumptions to be sure you are both in agreement.

» Ask how she goes about finding people with the attributes that matter to her. You might ask, "How do you verify these very subjective attribute that are so important to you?" The obvious answer is only through thorough reference checks.

» Once you and the manager have agreed that the only way of making sure that a candidate has certain attributes is through reference checks, you are ready to move on. However, you don't yet know if the manager will *use* a recruiter. You need to ask if a recruiter has been used in the past and what the experience was like, so you can overcome any objections or misconceptions the manager may have. Ask, "Mary, have you ever used a recruiter to fill a position?" If she answers in the affirmative, ask, "Was it a rewarding or a bad experience?" If it was a bad experience, I'd find out why it went bad so I could explain how I would overcome the problems and make it a rewarding experience.

» Once you believe the manager is comfortable with the concept of using you for finding a candidate who possesses all those intangibles, it is time to ask for a search assignment. Ask, "Do you have a current opening that I can help you with?" If not, "What are your hiring plans for the year?" If plans are uncertain, try, "It sounds like you need a little more time to solidify your hiring plans for the year. I'm going to check back with you in about a month to see if you have

a better idea of how things are going to go." (Remember to keep your name in front of managers. They will remember the reference checks, but they may not remember you unless you do something to remind them of who you are. Send a thank-you note, along with something with your name on it that they will keep.)

Thank both the peer and the manager for their evaluations. They have done a great service for you and your clients by being so cooperative and objective.

And, now that you've learned the fundamentals of the business, let's put a deal together.

CHAPTER 9

PUTTING THE DEAL TOGETHER

DON'T BE AFRAID
OF THE OPPOSITION.
REMEMBER, A KITE
RISES AGAINST,
NOT WITH THE WIND.

— HAMILTON WRIGHT MABIE

You have search assignments to fill and candidates to fill those search assignments. Now, it's time to put them together into a package that will earn you the fee you deserve. This is an area where some recruiters stumble because they haven't paid attention to all the details involved in "putting a deal together." After getting up and brushing themselves off, they scratch their heads and wonder why "a sure thing" went down the tubes.

The name of the game is "control." All sorts of things can go wrong if you lose control of the hiring process. Recruiters who work like an agency start out with no control, by sending resumés to human resource departments. If you have no control to begin with, you are going to be at the mercy of the gods of random distribution who decree that you stand in line with the sixty other recruiters who have no control of the hiring process and wait your turn for a placement. Everything we have discussed so far is intended to ensure that you do not have to deal with these gods of random distribution. By paying strict attention to how you put your deals together, your ratio of search assignments to placements will approach the goal of four placements for every five search assignments you undertake.

Begin to close the deal when you start taking the information about the search assignment from the hiring manager. The closer you can come to taking a search assignment in the manner described in Chapter 2, the more control you have over the hiring process and the more control you will have over who gets the placement. However, it is not always possible to take a search assignment in the ideal way. Sometimes, you are forced to work with human resources, and at other times you cannot commit to finding four good candidates who will be ready to interview by next Friday afternoon.

You can maximize your chances of a placement regardless of the circumstances under which you must work by following through on those processes over which you do have control. We've already discussed how to get the right candidates before the hiring manager for interviews. Now we must ensure that nothing is left to chance. You must learn how to orchestrate the interviews, the follow-ups, the offer, the counter-offer and everything else that can make or break the placement.

PREPARING FOR THE FIRST INTERVIEW

Hiring decisions are never made after the first interview. Decision-making is a process that occurs only after both the hiring manager and the candidate have had time to assess each other and the opportunity thoroughly. This process generally requires at least two, and sometimes several interviews, along with a good deal of guidance and follow-up on your part. You need to remain actively involved during the entire decision-making process.

We've already discussed how to prepare your candidate for the first interview. However, there are a few things that need to be re-emphasized. First and foremost, your candidate must thoroughly understand everything you've been able to gather about the position, the hiring manager and the company. I sometimes write up a brief dissertation about these things and hand it to my candidates, along with a suggestion that they go to the library and learn more about the company. One of the questions asked in every interview is, "Why do you want to come to work for our company?" The well-prepared candidate can talk with authority about the company's reputation, products, position in the market place and annual report. Such a candidate is sure to make a very positive impression. I also try to give candidates who've had scant interviewing experience information about how one prepares and sits for an interview.

A large percentage of the placements lost by recruiters result from misunderstandings over salaries. Companies, in general, don't know how to get salary requirements from a candidate. Candidates have no idea how to relay their salary requirements to a company. As a result, companies frequently make bad offers that the candidate has no option but to turn down. A recruiter should never let this happen.

There is no *good* way to ask what sort of salary expectations candidates have, or what sort of salary they are looking for, or how much they expect to make, or anything else that has to do with salary. There are only *bad* ways to ask these questions, so there can be only bad answers. Candidates attempting to answer questions about salary find themselves between a rock and a hard place. On the one hand, they want as much as they can get; on the other hand, they don't want to bid themselves out of a job, or look too greedy. Every candidate has a different reaction to the question and every reaction has a problem. Some candidates have told me that they asked for a ridiculously high salary because they thought that would send the hiring manager the message that they thought well of themselves. Others tell me they bid high because they believe the company will negotiate with them and they don't want to start the negotiations too low. No candidate wants to put down the lowest acceptable salary for fear that the company will assume that this can be negotiated lower still. And, of course, the candidate would prefer a salary that is higher than the lowest they are willing to accept.

For these reasons, I instruct my candidates never to discuss salary in the interview. I assure candidates that the salary range for the position is within the parameters we have agreed upon, and that they must let me negotiate the salary on their behalf. If they are required to fill out an application that asks for salary expectations, I tell them to write "open" in that space. If a candidate is asked point blank about salary expectations, I instruct my candidate to say, "Richard has assured me that the salary range for the position is within my salary requirements. My primary concern is to be sure that the position is what I am looking for and that I am what you are looking for. I am sure that if

those items are in place, you will make me an acceptable offer."

I am equally adamant with hiring managers. I let them know that the first interview should only be for purposes of determining if the candidate is right for the position and if the position is right for the candidate. I assure the manager that the salary expectations of all my candidates are within the salary range offered for the position and that the subject should not be broached with my candidates. I explain to the manager that there is no good way of asking the question and there is no good way of answering it. Nine times out of ten, asking the question only leads to a misunderstanding. Finally, I help my managers understand that they will be better served by letting me negotiate the salary issue after they have selected the candidate. I assure managers that I will negotiate an acceptable salary well within the salary framework we have agreed upon.

Before sending candidates off to an interview, instruct them to call you right after the interview is over. This is not an option. They must call. If a candidate wants to know why, say that you will be calling the manager right after the interview and you want to be able to relay his or her reaction (enthusiasm) about the company and position. Every manager looks more favorably upon a candidate who has expressed enthusiasm for the position and the company. Also, let your candidate know that you will get immediate feedback from the manager and you will want to relay that feedback. Not a soul in the world isn't curious about a manager's reaction. When candidates know they can get feedback by calling you right away, they'll call.

Prior to the interview, I make a commitment to the manager to provide immediate feedback from the candidate. This is something a manager seldom gets, but it is something every manager wants and needs. The manager will be equally concerned about how the interview went from the candidate's point of view, especially if the candidate was good. The manager would much rather extend an invitation for a follow-up interview to someone interested in the position than to someone whose interest is unknown.

First Follow-up

Human communication is imperfect and, no matter how hard both parties try, some muddled communication will occur during the interview. Part of your responsibility in putting the deal together is to discover where communication went awry during the interview and to straighten it out. This is another reason why it is so important that your candidate call you right away. First of all, you need to correct any misconceptions carried away from the interview. Second, you need to make sure that an unintended slight doesn't become a major issue over time. In today's climate of politically sensitive speech, it is difficult to avoid a verbal miscue in the course of a conversation lasting one to two hours.

Therefore, when your candidate calls you after the first interview, you need to ask a number of specific things. "How did things go?" just doesn't cut it in this business.

1. "How long did the interview last?"

Normally, the longer the interview, the better the prospects. If the interview isn't going well, one party or the other will usually try to shorten it. However, if the manager is committed to spending a maximum of an hour per interview, the length of the interview will not be much of an indicator of the success of the interview.

2. "Did you talk to any one else? Who?"

Normally, the first interview takes place with the hiring manager only. The purpose of this interview is to allow the manager to whittle the list of candidates down to a few finalists who will then be asked to come back and meet with others in the company. If your candidate is asked to meet with others during the first interview, it demonstrates a strong interest in your candidate, except of course if this other person had been previously scheduled to meet with your candidate.

3. "How did you and (the manager) get along? Is this someone you would feel comfortable working (with/for)?"

Here, you are fishing for objections or concerns about the manager. If the candidate feels uncomfortable about some aspect of the manager's behavior or attitude, you need to know it now, not when the company extends an offer to the candidate. If you wait until the offer is extended to find out there is a problem, it will be too late to correct it and the placement will evaporate.

4. "Is there anything you didn't understand about the position? Do you know what is required of someone who accepts the position?"

Nobody ever comes away from an interview with a complete grasp of the situation. Everyone's had the experience of leaving an intense conversation and later wishing he or she had asked several other questions or made several other points. Your candidate will also realize that certain questions were not fully answered.

Some of these questions will be matters of curiosity, while some will impact on the candidate's decision to pursue the position. You need to find out and immediately address those questions that will impact your candidate's decision to pursue the position.

5. "Do you feel you can handle all the challenges the position has to offer?"

   You really want to know if there is anything about the position that the candidate can't or doesn't want to deal with. The position may sound monotonous or repetitious. Your candidate may feel the position demands skills that he or she has not acquired. In either case, the concern or misconception might be due to imperfect communication. You need to find this out before the candidate drops from contention because of a misperception.

6. "What did you learn about the company?"

   Here, too, you want to find out if there are concerns about the company that might lead your candidate to reject the position.

7. "Do you have any other concerns about the position, the manager or the company that we haven't already talked about?"

   Make every effort to uncover and address all misperceptions. I once knew a recruiter who believed that if she didn't ask any questions a candidate's concerns would magically disappear. Unfortunately, it was she who eventually disappeared when all her placements fell apart.

Hard Question #1

If you get the feeling that your candidate is not communicating honestly with you or is holding back something that could make a difference in the outcome of the placement, you must ask The Hard Question. This question makes even the most reticent candidates reveal exactly where they stand. If you can, save this question until you are ready to close the deal, but sometimes it can't wait. Ask, "Would you accept this position if it were offered to you today?"

This may well force a "no" from your candidate. Then ask the question that will reveal your candidate's concerns: "Why not?"

At this point, whatever your candidate is holding back must come out. Most of the time, it is something that can be easily resolved and the placement process can continue. However, if you do not find out what the problem is, the deal will die.

First Follow-up Interview With the Hiring Manager

Armed with a good post-interview session with your candidate, you're now ready to talk with the hiring manager. You'll want:

» to relay the candidate's enthusiasm to the manager. This enthusiasm will have an impact on how the manager sees the candidate;

» to address any concerns the candidate had so they can be clarified;

» to get the manager's reaction to the interview and the candidate.

You might start the follow-up interview this way:

You: "I had an opportunity to talk with John at length about the interview. He indicated that you two spent about an hour and a half together. Is that about right?"

Manager: "Yes."

You: "John came away feeling very good about the whole process. He likes your company and he likes the position and the responsibilities it involves. He feels comfortable that he has the experience necessary to handle all the requirements of the position and, at the same time, the position is sophisticated enough to offer him a solid challenge and some great learning opportunities. He was especially impressed with your management style. He felt that you both had the same philosophical approach to the various assignments and problems your section is facing. This is very important to him. He also had a couple of small concerns I need to go over with you, but they just need clarification and will not impact his desire to continue to pursue the position. John's perception was that you two could work well together. Did you get the same feeling?"

From here, you will pretty much follow the same process you followed with John. Your primary goal is to discover any objections or misconceptions the manager might have that could prevent the process from moving to completion. You might ask these questions:

» "John felt he fit the position very well. Do you have any concerns about how John would do in the position?"

» "Do you think John had a good grasp of what the position would require of him?"

» "John seemed to think he would thrive in your environment. Do you foresee any problems for him?"

Hard Question #2

Once again, there is a *Hard Question* you can ask if you feel the manager is not giving you an honest appraisal of the interview and the candidate. In this case the Hard Question is: "Can I tell John that you are interested in making him an offer of employment at this time?"

If the response is "no," then you can ask, "Why not?" Regardless of how you get all the concerns out in the open, you must do one of two things:

1. Make arrangements with the manager and the candidate for the second interview; or

2. Clear up whatever concerns are expressed and then arrange for the second interview.

Obviously, if there are concerns to be handled, additional phone calls will be necessary. Let your candidate know the manager's responses to any concerns. Assuming the responses are satisfactory, you can then make arrangements with the candidate for the second interview. Once the candidate's concerns have been addressed, you are ready to go through the same exercise with the manager.

Follow-up to Second Interview

The second and, if necessary, subsequent interviews usually entail the candidate (let's use Brenda this time) meeting with others within the company. For the most part, Brenda will meet people with whom she will likely have a good deal of contact. In effect, the manager has decided Brenda can handle the position and wants the others to approve. If anyone doesn't feel comfortable with her, this is an opportunity to say so before she is hired. This lets the manager off the hook in the event one of these key people encounters problems afterwards.

If you've done your job following the first

interview, all of Brenda's concerns about the position will have been successfully handled, and she will not have any specific concerns following the second interview, unless there is someone she just can't abide. Although this seldom happens, any such concern should be immediately relayed to the hiring manager. Often there's a misconception that can be corrected, but sometimes your candidate could get "blackballed" by one of the interviewers. This is not a frequent occurrence, but it can happen. The more people there are to be seen, the more likely it will be that someone will object to your candidate.

Make it a policy to insist that the manager bring back at least two candidates for a second interview. Although the manager may have a clear favorite, there's no guarantee that everything will go smoothly during the second interview. Therefore, it makes sense to have a second, or even a third candidate go through the process just in case something happens to the manager's first choice. The manager has lost nothing by bringing back two additional finalists. There's no need to risk repeating the entire recruiting and interviewing process.

PREPARING FOR THE OFFER

If not earlier, then certainly by the time the second interview has been completed, you will know if Brenda is interested enough in the position to consider a reasonable offer. At this point, your responsibility is to move the candidate from a willingness to consider an offer to granting you permission to accept an offer on her behalf. To do this, Brenda must agree to two things:

» She must want the position.

» You must agree on an acceptable salary.

What we want the most is often what we can't have. The very best recruiters know this instinctively. Some candidates think that by playing coy and hard to get, they will enhance their value. Don't allow your candidate to play this game. If Tom shows reluctance to commit to a position, a good recruiter will take the position away from him. The conversation should go something like this:

Recruiter: "It doesn't sound to me like you have any real interest in the position. Perhaps I should call Ms. Smith and ask to withdraw your name from consideration as a candidate for the position."

Candidate: "Wait a minute. Don't do that. I just wanted some more time to think about it."

Recruiter: "I thought we had pretty well covered all your concerns about the position and the company. You need to make up your mind. I have an obligation to let Mary know one way or the other, so she can consider other candidates if there is any question about your interest in the position."

Candidate: "I guess you can go ahead and tell her I'm very interested."

Recruiter: "Are you sure? I don't want to be embarrassed by having you back out on me later."

Candidate: "Yes. I'm sure."

You might think that a conversation like this might scare the candidate away, and you're right. However, if it does scare the candidate away, the placement had no chance to begin with. It's better to find out right away that your candidate is not sold on a position so that you can proceed with other candidates. You certainly don't want to find out that there's no real interest by having your candidate suddenly turn down an offer. You're going to look rather foolish if you encourage a manager to extend an offer that is subsequently turned down. Your commitment, after all, is to the manager who is paying your fee.

Once the candidate has made a commitment to accept the position, you are ready to get a commitment from the manager. Generally, if the candidate has passed muster with everyone during the second interview, the manager is ready to make an offer. Your job at this point is to assure the manager that the candidate is ready to accept a reasonable offer and to confirm that an offer from the company is forthcoming. However, you do not want the offer yet. You still need to negotiate the salary with the candidate and the manager. This is where you can become a hero to both parties if you negotiate properly.

NEGOTIATING THE SALARY

You need to establish three specific thresholds with the candidate and the manager. For the candidate the three thresholds are:

1. The lowest salary the candidate would even be willing to consider;

2. The lowest salary the candidate would, however reluctantly, accept;

3. The lowest salary the candidate would consider a great offer.

Let's assume the hiring range for a position is between $30,000 and $40,000. A conversa-

tion with Candidate Sally Michaels might go something like this:

Recruiter: "I know the company is interested in making you an offer, and I want to make sure it is an appropriate offer, one that you will be happy with. Would you be willing to accept an offer of $30,000?"

Sally: "Oh, no. That's too low. That's less than I'm making now."

Recruiter: "I realize that, but we don't want the company to think that your only motivation for joining them is financial. How about $32,000? Would you consider something in that order?"

Sally: "Probably not."

Recruiter: "If I could get you $33,000, would you accept that?"

Sally: "Possibly. I'd have to think about it." (You have now uncovered *Threshold #1.*)

Recruiter: "If I could get you an offer of $34,000, could I accept the offer on your behalf?"

Sally: "Yeah. I suppose so, although I think I'm worth $35,000. However, there is a lot of opportunity there and I'm not going to quibble over a thousand dollars." (You have now established *Thresholds #2 and #3*. The candidate would accept $34,000 and would be delighted with $35,000.)

Once you have established the thresholds for the candidate, you are ready to establish these same thresholds with the hiring manager. However, in this case the scenario operates in reverse.

Recruiter: "Sally has expressed a strong interest in joining your company. I think she is ready to accept a good offer. Would you be willing to offer her $40,000?"

Manager: "Oh, no. I couldn't do that. It would be unfair to my more experienced employees who are making less than that."

Recruiter: "Do you think you could offer $38,000? Sally is a pretty good candidate. I know I could get her to accept $38,000."

Manager: "I don't know. I'd have to think about it." *(Threshold #1)*

Recruiter: "How about $37,000. I would have to have the candidate's permission to accept such an offer but I think I can get her to agree to $37,000."

Manager: "We could probably do that although I had something a little less in mind." *(Threshold #2)*

Recruiter: "I'm going to try for $36,000. I know Sally really wants the position. If I can't get her to take $36,000, do I have your permission to offer $37,000?"

Manager: "$36,000 would be great if you can get her to accept it." *(Threshold #3)* "If not, I guess we can go $37,000."

You can now go back to your candidate with an offer you know is more than acceptable. You will be a hero to the candidate with an offer of $35,500. That's $1,500 more than she expected and $500 more than her best expectations.

The manager will be elated when you announce that you got the candidate to accept an offer of $35,500. This will take a great burden off the manager who was wondering how to explain to his other employees why this candi-

date was getting $37,000.

It's nice to be a hero to both the candidate and the manager, and there's no reason why you shouldn't be. You earned it. While other recruiters will pray that things work out, you made sure they did.

Giving Notice

You have definitely won the toughest battle, but the war is not yet over. You need to make sure there is agreement as to when the candidate will start the new position. Once that is determined, you need to escort the candidate through the process of giving notice to his or her current employer.

There is no legal reason why the candidate could not start working at the new position the very next day. However, protocol dictates that employees give employers two weeks' notice of their intent to leave. Therefore, it is best all around to target a date that will allow for this two weeks' notice. It's also nicer to start a new position on a Monday, although there is no requirement that this occur. Therefore, establishing a starting date of two weeks from the following Monday is usually satisfactory for everyone. This gives the candidate an opportunity to sever all ties to the old company and enjoy the weekend before starting with the new company. Likewise, it gives the hiring manager an opportunity to put together an orientation program for the new employee that will start at the beginning of a week.

Before you help the candidate give notice, make sure the candidate has no unfinished business with the current employer. Now that your candidate fully realizes that he or she is about to embark upon a new career opportunity with another company, several problems can arise. There may be a project that needs to be completed, so the current employer isn't left in a lurch. There may be a week's vacation due, an annual bonus that could be lost if a month's notice isn't given, etc. These are valid concerns that need to be respected. It does little good to chastise the candidate for not thinking of these things sooner. After all, it is your job to tie up loose ends. Make sure all the bases are covered before you determine the actual start date.

Where the candidate is concerned about an unfinished project, it shows an admirable level of integrity that the hiring manager will appreciate. However, it is your responsibility to make sure the candidate understands he or she is not indispensable at the current place of employment. A suitable replacement will be found. An employee cannot complete everything that's been assigned, so a specific goal that can be reached within two or three weeks should be identified. The goal should be geared toward helping one's successor take over. Anything else is unacceptable. The candidate has, after all, made a commitment to the new company and new manager.

Most candidates are unaware that earned vacation time cannot be taken away from them just because they decide to leave the company. They are entitled to take that earned vacation and, should they leave before taking it, the company must pay them in cash for it. It's the law. The candidate must decide whether to take the cash and live on it for a week before starting a new job, or take the cash, put it in the bank and start the new job immediately. The recruiter should be involved in this decision since it will impact the starting date. The hiring manager needs to be kept informed as well.

If the candidate is due to receive a bonus in the next two or three weeks, the hiring manager must accept the delay. No one can be expected to forfeit several thousand dollars. The only reasonable option the manager has is to offer to compensate the candidate for the loss. If the bonus will delay the start date for more then a month, however, the candidate should take the loss. This is really seldom an issue, since an employee normally doesn't begin looking for employment until after the bonus for that year has been distributed.

Once the start date has been established, your next responsibility is to help the candidate give notice of resigning. This should be timed so that the candidate gives the current company no more and no less than the normal two weeks' notice. If the start date is Monday, May 18th, then the notice should be given on either Friday, May 1st or Monday, May 4th.

Most candidates have had little experience in giving notice and tend to make far too much of it. Therefore, I try to coach them to make it as simple as possible. It should always be in writing. I suggest that they set it up something like this:

```
Dear (boss' name):

I have accepted a position with an-
other company. My last day with XYZ
Company will be on Friday, May 15,
1994. I am requesting that my final
paycheck along with my earned vaca-
tion pay be ready for me on that
day.

Sincerely,

Roger Brown
```

At this point, if he feels so inclined, Roger is free to tell his current boss how wonderful it was to work there and how sad it is to leave. The important thing is to be sure that the actual resignation is properly addressed.

After you and Roger have agreed on a date and time to submit the resignation to his current boss, tell him that you will be calling immediately afterward to make sure no unforeseen problems have arisen. Your job, after all, is to help your candidate through any rough spots. In reality, the knowledge that you will be calling will keep your candidate from getting cold feet at the last minute.

THE COUNTER-OFFER

Before you can begin to relax, make sure your candidate is fully aware of the dangers of a counter-offer from the old company. A counter-offer is any inducement offered by a current employer to get a resigning employee to reconsider leaving the company. Inform your candidate that there are thousands of documented cases that clearly demonstrate why a person should *never* accept a counter-offer!

Investigations of employers and the experiences of employees who have accepted counter-offers reveal that, in almost every instance, acceptance is invariably the road to career suicide. Studies over a period of twenty-five years reveal that candidates who accept counter-offers rarely benefit from them. On the other hand, companies always benefit from them; otherwise, the company wouldn't offer them.

Let's look at counter-offers realistically.

When employees quit, it is a direct reflection on their managers. Managers' gut reactions will be to keep employees from leaving until they're good and ready. Often, this means keeping someone until an appropriate replacement is found, at which point the manager quite gleefully dumps an employee who, out of misguided loyalty, had accepted a counter-offer.

In an article for the *National Business Employment Weekly* (December 11, 1983), Paul Hawkinson, for many years a successful recruiter and consultant, listed some of the things that might go through a manager's mind when an employee decides to leave:

» "This couldn't happen at a worse time."

» "This is one of my best people. If I let him quit now, it'll wreak havoc on the morale of the department."

» "I've already got one opening [in] my department. I don't need another right now."

» "This will probably screw up the entire vacation schedule."

» "I'm working as hard as I can, and I don't need to do his work, too."

» "If I lose another good employee, the company might decide to 'lose' me, too."

» "My review is coming up and this will make me look bad."

» "Maybe I can keep him on until I find a suitable replacement."

None of these thoughts include any concern about the status of the employee who is leaving. And why should it? My old boss used to suggest to all her candidates that they should consider a resignation the employee's way of firing the company. To understand how the company might feel about an employee's

133

resignation, just think how it would feel if the company fired you.

Counter-offers come in all sizes and shapes. The company may be willing to promise anything, since most of the promises are only intended to keep the resigning employee on hand until an appropriate replacement can be found.

Early in my recruiting career, I had a young man interview for a position that would considerably enhance his career. When Sam got back to work, he told his boss about his interview. His boss and another manager took Sam out to lunch and begin painting a beautiful picture of how he was going to advance if he stayed put. Sam called to let me know that there was advancement awaiting him where he was currently working and that he didn't need to look elsewhere. That led to the following conversation:

Me: "How many people are there in your group?"

Sam: "Fourteen."

Me: "How many of them started working for the company before you did?"

Sam: "Eleven."

Me: "How do you think those eleven are going to feel if you get promoted over their heads? Do you think they'll stick around?"

It took him about ten seconds to realize he had been played for a fool by his boss. He was soon working for my client.

Paul Hawkinson goes on to suggest these universal truths about counter-offers:

» Any situation in which an employee is forced to get an outside offer before the present employer will suggest a raise, promotion or better working conditions, is suspect.

» No matter what the company says when making its counter-offer, you will always be considered a fidelity risk. Having once demonstrated your lack of loyalty (for whatever reason), you will lose your status as a team player and your place in the inner circle.

» Counter-offers are usually nothing more than stall devices to give your employer time to replace you.

» Your reasons for wanting to leave still exist. Conditions are just made a bit more tolerable in the short term because of the raise, promotion or promises made to keep you.

» Counter-offers are only made in response to a threat to quit. Will you have to solicit an offer and threaten to quit every time you deserve better working conditions?

» Decent and well-managed companies don't make counter-offers. Ever! Their policies are fair and equitable. They will not be subjected to counter-offer coercion or what they perceive as blackmail.

If, after hearing all this, your candidate is still considering a counter-offer, perhaps you should recommend psychiatric counseling. Your final responsibility to your candidate and client is to stay in contact with them from time to time. Make sure things are going well during the two-week period after the candidate has given notice, and for the first three months the candidate is on the new job.

Now let's talk about fees and guarantees.

CHAPTER 10

FEES AND GUARANTEES

WHY NOT GO OUT
ON A LIMB?
ISN'T THAT WHERE
THE FRUIT IS?

FRANK SCULLY

Misconceptions about fees and guarantees abound within the recruiting world. These misconceptions exist in the minds of hiring managers, human resource personnel, and many recruiters as well.

The Contingency Fee

Most recruiters work on a contingency basis. That is, they do all the work up front without any assurance of getting paid. They only receive payment if the client decides to hire their candidate. This is not unlike lawyers who accept lawsuits on a contingency basis. A lawyer is not likely to accept a case unless there is a good likelihood of winning, and neither should a recruiter.

This may seem like an unrewarding way to work, but it has several advantages for the recruiter. Much like the contingency fee a lawyer receives, a contingency fee for a recruiter is generally much higher than a regular fee for service assignment. When the recruiter takes on a contingency assignment, no money is exchanged and there is, therefore, no commitment. If the recruiter decides to abandon a search for whatever reason, there is no financial commitment to continue. Finally, when you agree to work on a contingency basis, you have much more freedom to dictate the terms of the assignment.

If you were to examine the contingency fees advertised in the brochures of most recruiting firms, you would find that almost all firms have the same fee schedules. The fee they charge their clients is determined by charging a percentage of the annual salary offered to the candidate the client hires. Most fee schedules look something like this:

If the candidate's starting annual salary is / **The fee will be**

	to	$19,999	20% of the salary
$20,000	to	$20,999	21% of the salary
$21,000	to	$21,999	22% of the salary
$22,000	to	$22,999	23% of the salary
$23,000	to	$23,999	24% of the salary
$24,000	to	$24,999	25% of the salary
$25,000	to	$25,999	26% of the salary
$26,000	to	$26,999	27% of the salary
$27,000	to	$27,999	28% of the salary
$28,000	to	$28,999	29% of the salary
$29,00	and over		30% of the salary

In other words, if the client offers your candidate an annual salary of $35,000, your fee would be 30% of that $35,000, or $10,500. There are many things wrong with this system, but clients have accepted it, and such things are hard to change. In the late 1980s several recruiting firms moved their top percentage to 35%, and before the 1990-1993 recession a few were collecting 35% fees. However, most firms stayed at the 30% level.

The development of a progressive fee schedule was predicated on the assumption that the more skilled the professional (the more highly paid), the more difficult that person would be to recruit. While this is not totally unfounded, the perception is riddled with exceptions. Nevertheless, the perception exists, and you should use it to your best advantage. I doubt that in today's market place there is a single professional with two or more years' experience making less than $30,000. Therefore, if everyone were paid in accordance with the fee schedule in the adjacent column, no fee would ever be under $9,000 (30% of $30,000). One of the problems with the progressive fee schedule is that a person with two years' experience is generally harder to find and recruit than someone with more experience. Therefore, you get a higher fee for recruiting the more easily recruited person.

The fee schedules were established over twenty years ago and have remained virtually unchanged. In the mid '70s, a highly qualified professional might make $20,000, and the fee for recruiting that person would run about $4,000 (20% of $20,000). Inflation has brought this same professional's salary to $80,000 or better. Therefore, using the fee schedule developed in the '70s, the fee for recruiting the same professional in 1992 would be $24,000 (30% of $80,000).

In this example, the salary of the professional increased fourfold, but the fee for recruiting that professional increased sixfold. This discrepancy has not gone unnoticed by most client companies. However, rather than attempt to change a twenty-year-old tradition, they have developed their own fee policy. Many client companies have arbitrarily set a maximum fee for the recruiting services of any recruiter regardless of the position. Most have set this maximum fee at either 20% or 25%, although a few will still pay 30%. This makes even less sense than the schedule currently in use by most recruiters. However, neither system has any relationship to the time and costs a recruiter incurs when filling a position.

Because the current fee system doesn't make a whole lot of sense, I set a fee that is fair without taking advantage of the client or short-changing myself. I will often take on an assignment for a flat fee. This means that my fee will not be tied to the candidate's salary but, instead, to the effort I put into placing the candidate. Most clients think this is a great idea. I usually establish the flat fee by averaging the fee I would collect if the candidate were hired at either the highest end or lowest end of the salary range. For example, if the salary range for the position is between $35,000 and $45,000 and the fee rate would have been 25%, my fee might be anywhere between $8,750 and $11,250. I then calculate my flat fee by averaging the highest and lowest fee. In this case, my flat fee would be exactly $10,000. Clients always want to hire the best candidate, which means that they will most likely pay a fee near the $11,250 mark. I think it is unfair to penalize a client for hiring the best candidate. I tell the client that it's unfair and that I will work at a flat rate so my fee won't influence their decision to hire the best candidate.

What Are They Paying For?

Ask most clients what they're paying a recruiter for and you probably won't get a satisfactory answer. Human resource people might say they're paying for selected resumés. Hiring managers might say they're paying for you to recruit a top candidate from a competitor's company. Even some recruiters might say they're being paid to recruit the right candidate for a client. Were any of these answers true, these people should be very angry.

If human resources is right, the recruiter does nothing but review a few files, call a few people and spend a few dollars mailing resumés to earn a $10,000 fee. The whole shebang probably takes three hours, tops. That's about $3,330 per hour. Who wouldn't hate to pay a recruiter that kind of money?

If the hiring manager is right, a recruiter spends about twenty hours hunting down and persuading an exceptional candidate to defect to the manager's company. That puts the recruiter in the neighborhood of $500.00 per hour, a rather enviable neighborhood. What's important is not the misconception but the negative effect such a perception can have on the relationship between client and recruiter. Most human resources personnel and many managers sincerely believe they are being ripped off by greedy recruiters.

In order to feel that they are getting their money's worth, human resources personnel and most hiring managers will grant the search assignment to many different recruiting agencies, the rationale being that, if they are going to pay $10,000 for a candidate, they should have at least twenty people working on the assignment. To them, this not only increases the odds of getting the very best candidate, it makes it easier to accept paying a $10,000 fee. Unfortunately, this not only costs the client a lot of extra time and money, it also perpetuates a system that breeds incompetence.

I don't like people to think that I'm ripping them off, so I make every effort to help my clients understand what they're paying for. I let them know that I've been working on this search assignment for the ten years it took me to build the database of candidates they will have access to. If I get a fee of $10,000, they will have only paid me a dollar an hour to build that database. Moreover, I will be providing them with many other services as well:

» I will be saving them a considerable amount of time and money by screening the hundreds of candidates in my database so as to send them only the most qualified.

» I will save them money and time by making sure that the interview process is efficient and productive.

» I will make sure they don't waste time on candidates who aren't really interested in the position or on candidates whose salary expectations are out of line.

» I will make sure that they don't have to repeat the entire hiring process a second time as a result of having made an unacceptable offer or having courted an uninterested candidate.

» I will save them money by negotiating the lowest salary the candidate is willing to accept.

» I will make sure the candidate has no second thoughts about resigning from his or her current position.

» I will make sure the candidate will not succumb to a counter-offer from the current employer.

» I will continue to check with the candidate and the hiring manager for at least three months after the candidate starts work at the new position to make sure no unanticipated problems have arisen. There is no requirement that I do this; I just consider it good public relations. Nothing gives a manager more confidence in a recruiter than a periodic call from that recruiter checking to see that the candidate is working out well.

When all of this is considered, I believe I have earned my fee. That I have been building a database of candidates for the past ten years is a bonus clients get for selecting me as their recruiter.

NEGOTIATING THE FEE

Understanding what you are being paid for puts you in a much better position to negotiate a reasonable fee. Obviously, the client would like to pay as little as possible while having access to your database and your services. Having confidence in the services you offer, your client will help you negotiate your fee.

When clients ask what my fees are, I tell them that my fees are the same as those charged by most agencies; that is, 30% of the candidate's annual salary for the first year. Occasionally, a client will accept that and my work begins. More often, I get one of three responses:

1. "That's too much. Are you willing to negotiate?"

2. "Our company has a policy of only paying X%."

3. "Other agencies are willing to work on the assignment for just X%."

I am delighted to respond to these objections. They allow me to negotiate some terms I might not otherwise get. I would much rather have a search assignment where I dictate the terms of the search for a 20% fee than to have a search assignment with a 30% fee where I have little or no say as to how the search is conducted. Making a placement is virtually assured when I can dictate the terms. Here's how I would deal with these objections:

1. When a client says, "That's too much. Are you willing to negotiate?" they are usually asking if I am willing to lower my fees. However, negotiation involves a willingness for each side to give a little here and there. Therefore, I use the bargaining chips the client has to offer, even though the client might not be aware of them. One bargaining chip the client has is exclusivity. First, I'll ask for exclusivity as a condition for lowering my fee. In the event the manager has already given the search assignment to other agencies, I put their second bargaining chip on the table. I tell the manager I will reduce my fee if he or she will set aside one afternoon to interview my four best candidates. After all, having this kind of control over the hiring process is almost as good as having an exclusive.

Judgment plays a critical role in the recruiting business. It's just as important to know when to walk away from an assignment that has little placement potential as it is to work on an assignment with lots of placement potential. The successful recruiter is the one who can tell a manager, "I'm sorry, but I don't think it would be in my best interest to work on this assignment under the conditions you have described. I could go ahead and accept the assignment, but I would only be misleading you:

You would not be receiving my best efforts and this is not fair to either of us."

2. "Our company has a policy of only paying X%" is in many ways similar to the one above. The difference is that the manager has already set the fee lower than your standard fee of 30% before negotiations have even begun. Your response would change only in its approach, and you might engage in the following conversation:

You: "You are asking me to cut my fee by one-third. What can I expect in return for cutting my fee?"

Manager: "What do you mean?"

You: "If I cut my fee by one-third, would you be willing to give me an exclusive?"

From here, the bargaining follows the same path we took in responding to the first objection. If the manager has already given the search assignment to other recruiters, you can demand that an afternoon be set aside to interview your four best candidates. You'll find that the manager will bend over backwards to give you some advantage over other recruiters. You have demonstrated that you are someone special, that you have a good deal of confidence in your ability, and the manager will want to find a way of working with you. This is not unlike the situation where we pulled the position away from the wishy-washy candidate in the last chapter. Everyone wants what they can't have. If the manager thinks you are pulling out, he or she will try to find a way to work with you.

3. Hearing that "other agencies are willing to work on the assignment for just X%," I generally respond, "You get what you pay for."

Your conversation might go like this:

You: "Were they honest enough to tell you what you will be getting for your reduced fee?"

Manager: "What do you mean?"

You: "When I accept an assignment at a reduced fee, I make sure my client knows what they are asking for. Not all agencies are that honest."

Manager: "I don't understand."

You: "I'm sure that, like me, the other recruiters have clients looking for the same candidate you are seeking. If the other clients are paying full fees, they'll get first crack at the best candidates. The other agencies probably didn't tell you, but you are most likely getting the leftovers."

Here's a prospect the client hadn't previously considered. Like most of us, they took such pride in negotiating a better price they forgot about the product. You get what you pay for. Now that you have the manager on the ropes, there are several directions you can take. Since you already know there are other firms working on the assignment, you can't ask for an exclusive. However, you will certainly have no trouble convincing that client to see your four *best* candidates during an afternoon of your choosing.

If the proffered fee is ridiculously low, say 15%, you might issue a challenge much like I did with a particularly stubborn manager. I told the manager that I never work for less than 30% because my candidates were well worth my fee, but I offered the following challenge. If he would set aside an hour and a half of his time the following Wednesday afternoon I would let him interview my best candidate. If he agreed

that mine was the best candidate, he would pay me the standard 30% fee. If mine was not the best candidate, I would formally apologize and he would never hear from me again. I got my 30% fee, and the manager understood what I meant when I'd told him he was getting the leftovers from other recruiters. There *are* recruiters who are only worth a 15 or 20% fee, but I'm not one of them. I don't want you to be one of them either.

THE GUARANTEE

I'm not sure how the concept of a guarantee got started, but it has become the biggest farce in the recruiting business. Obviously, any client who has invested $10,000 or $15,000 in a new employee wants to protect that investment. And, unfortunately, there have been (and continue to be) some unscrupulous recruiters in the business. Concerns about money and ethics led clients to demand some form of guarantee from the recruiter. That's understandable, but now many clients are asking for something completely unreasonable.

This demand, like so many unreasonable demands, arose out of fear. The client feared that some money-hungry recruiters would lie about a candidate's background and references just to get a quick placement. Clients also feared that a recruiter would place a good candidate with their company, then spirit the candidate away as soon as the recruiter got paid, so the candidate could be placed elsewhere for another fee. Undoubtedly, there have been incidents where this very thing has happened. Such episodes are rare but, just like government regulations, everyone gets regulated because of one or two bad apples. In response to these fears, most recruiters adopted a policy of granting an across-the-board, unconditional thirty-day guarantee on all placements.

Basically, the recruiting industry has said to companies, "We will either find a replacement or refund your money if anything happens to the candidate within thirty days of the time the candidate starts to work for you. We don't care if the candidate is killed in an auto accident or is fired by you, we will take responsibility for that first thirty days."

I never was enthusiastic about this thirty-day guarantee because it didn't make sense to me. After all, while I gave clients information about candidates, I didn't make the hiring decision. They did. Why should I guarantee that they made the right decision? However, I went along with it because it seemed to be an industry standard. Besides, in my ten years of recruiting I've only had to replace one candidate. He died of a heart attack on his 22nd day. Nevertheless, I've always had problems accepting the principal of protecting clients from their own mistakes.

In recent years, certain clients have requested that the guarantee be extended to sixty or ninety days, and a few even asked for a six month guarantee. That's when my sense of justice takes over and my sense of generosity retreats. When someone asks for an extended guarantee, the conversation might go something like this:

You: "What am I supposed to guarantee?"

Client: "That the candidate will stay for at least ninety days."

You: "I'll do that on one condition."

Client: "What's that?"

You: "Make me president of your company."

Client: "Don't be silly. I can't do that."

You: "Well, how else am I going to guarantee that you won't have a layoff, or that you'll meet your payroll obligations or that you'll give my candidate the support needed to do a good job?"

Client: "We're not talking about things like that. Obviously, we wouldn't expect you to be responsible for those things."

You: "Well, why else would somebody leave your employment after only ninety days?"

Client: "I'm talking about a situation where we might have to let the candidate go because it turns out that he doesn't have the right skills or something."

You: "I see. You want me to guarantee that you made the right hiring decision. I'll tell you what. I'll do better than that. I'll guarantee every bit of the information I provide you with that influences your hiring decision, and not just for ninety days but for a whole year. Does that sound fair?"

Client: "I only need a ninety-day guarantee."

From this conversation, it's obvious that the request for an extended guarantee is a knee-jerk reaction by a client who has paid out large sums of money for talented candidates and then lost them. A natural reaction is to protect the investment by laying the responsibility on the recruiter. However, this does nothing to solve the real problem. A company that is losing good employees needs to do some hard self-examination. A recruiter who perpetuates the extended guarantee concept by accepting such a demand at face value is doing neither the client nor the recruiting industry any good. The problem of employees leaving can only be resolved by making the company face up to its own short comings.

THE CONTRACT

Once you and a client have agreed upon the fee and the guarantee, everything should be confirmed in writing. This amounts to nothing more than sending the client a letter spelling out the terms you and the client have agreed upon. Some people have questioned whether a letter from the recruiter is sufficient to make the agreement a binding contract. This has been tested in court on numerous occasions, and the recruiter has always won. The court has ruled that once a client has interviewed the recruiter's candidate, the client has demonstrated acceptance of the conditions described in the letter.

A few agencies insist that the client return a signed copy of the agreement. However, if a client decides not to pay, for whatever reason, a signed letter won't change the situation. Should the disagreement end up in court, the court's decision will still be predicated upon whether the client agreed to the contract by interviewing a recruiter's candidate.

It's important that you know where you stand legally, not that I expect you'll have trouble getting your clients to pay your fee. In my ten years as a recruiter, I have only had to file a court complaint against one client and as soon as that client received notice of my threatened court action, he paid up. Most companies are honest and more than willing to meet their financial obligations.

Recruiters usually have two or three standard form letters they use when sending a contract letter to their clients. You can use any form you'd like. A few that I normally use are reproduced here. The first is for clients that do not request any guarantee. The second is for clients requesting the traditional thirty-day guarantee. The third is for clients who insist on an extended guarantee.

You will notice that the longer the guarantee period, the higher the fee. By making sure the guarantee exempts me from any responsibility for the actions of the client, I can provide as long a time period as I like. The things I guarantee will not change over time. The information I provided the client about the candidate that the client used to make the hiring decision will be the same now and five years from now. However, the demand for a longer guarantee by the client gives me plenty of ammunition for negotiating a higher fee. "You want a longer guarantee. What will you give me in exchange?" In effect, the client in the last letter paid an extra $4,500 for a guarantee that is basically worthless.

LETTER OF AGREEMENT WITHOUT GUARANTEES

Date
Ms. Jane Doe
XYZ Company
Address
City, State, Zip

Dear Jane:

Thank you for the opportunity to assist you in locating candidates for the position of _____.

Please be assured that there will be no fee obligation on your part unless we provide a candidate you actually hire. When this occurs, our fee will be 20% of the candidate's annual salary for the first year. For example, if the candidate's salary for the first year is $45,000 the fee will be 20% of $45,000 or $9,000.

We again thank you for the opportunity to work with you on this assignment and look forward to a long business relationship with XYZ Company.

Sincerely,

Richard A. Mackie

LETTER OF AGREEMENT WITH 30-DAY GUARANTEE

Date
Ms. Jane Doe
XYZ Company
Address
City, State, Zip

Dear Jane:

Thank you for the opportunity to assist you in locating candidates for the position of _____

Please be assured that there will be no fee obligation on your part unless we provide a candidate you actually hire. When this occurs, our fee will be 25% of the candidate's salary for the first year. For example, if the candidate's salary for the first year is $45,000 the fee will be 25% of $45,000 or $11,250.

In addition, we are providing you with an unconditional guarantee that if the candidate should leave your employment at any time within the first thirty days, for any reason whatsoever, we will provide a replacement free of charge.

We again thank you for the opportunity to work with you on this assignment and look forward to a long business relationship with XYZ Company.

Sincerely,

Richard A. Mackie

LETTER OF AGREEMENT WITH EXTENDED GUARANTEE

Date
Ms. Jane Doe
XYZ Company
Address
City, State, Zip

Dear Jane:

Thank you for the opportunity to assist you in locating candidates for the position of_____

Please be assured that there will be no fee obligation on your part unless we provide a candidate you actually hire. When this occurs, our fee will be 30% of the expected annual compensation of the candidate. For example, if you hire our candidate at an annual compensation of $45,000, our fee would be 30% of the compensation or $13,500.

In accordance with your discussion with Richard Mackie, we further agree to modify our guarantee policy as follows:

If the candidate is terminated or leaves your employment within ninety days after the date of start, R. Mackie Associates will locate a replacement at no additional cost. Please note that we have also agreed that the guarantee policy will not apply if the candidate leaves under the following conditions:

1. The candidate is laid off.
2. XYZ Company fails to meet payroll.
3. XYZ fails to meet commitments made to the candidate.
4. XYZ misrepresents either the company or the position.
5. Any other action by XYZ that neither the candidate nor R.

Mackie Associates can control and that has a direct negative impact on the candidate's ability to continue as an employee of xyz Company.

Again, we appreciate the opportunity to work with you on this assignment and look forward to a long business relationship with xyz Company.

Sincerely,

Richard A. Mackie

And, now that you know what the recruiting business is all about, it's time to set up your own business.

CHAPTER 11

STARTING YOUR BUSINESS

HE WHO EVERY MORNING
PLANS THE TRANSACTION
OF THE DAY AND
FOLLOWS OUT THAT PLAN,
CARRIES A THREAD THAT
WILL GUIDE HIM
THROUGH THE MAZE OF
THE MOST BUSY LIFE. BUT
WHERE NO PLAN IS LAID,
WHERE THE DISPOSAL OF
TIME IS SURRENDERED
MERELY TO THE CHANCE
OF INCIDENCE, CHAOS
WILL SOON REIGN.

— VICTOR HUGO

One problem with most new businesses is that they cost a small fortune to get started. This is not true of the recruiting business. Obviously there may be things you might like to have, but only a few things are essential. We'll look at what you need to be functional, some options and some frills.

Location

Two options are available in locating your office. One is to rent space in a community office environment, the other is to have your office at home. Obviously, an office at home will be less expensive than renting an office. However, a home office may be less convenient to certain services that are available in an office setting. Consider the following in choosing where to set up your business:

1. A rented office setting might include a receptionist who answers the phone for you and greets your visitors.

2. There might be conference rooms available

where you can meet with clients and candidates.

3. Many office clusters have copying machines and a fax machine available to all renters.

4. Many clusters offer some form of typing service.

5. The rented office setting lends your business a professional appearance.

Renting an office offers less tangible services that should definitely be taken into consideration:

6. If you have an office to go to in the morning, you will be much more apt to get up, dress nicely, and go to work.

7. An office environment provides discipline to put in a full day's work. When working at home, it is easy to be distracted by a favorite television program or a screaming child who needs your immediate attention.

8. The rented office also gives you a chance to meet with and learn from other small business owners.

Renting an office could cost between $400 and $800 per month depending on where you live and how swanky an office you want. If you are making a placement a month as you planned, five or six hundred a month is small change. However, when you first start out, you might be living within a meager budget. An office on the fifty-fifth floor of a new skyscraper in downtown New York or San Francisco will cost quite a bit, and if you need something that spiffy, you might as well work for a recruiting agency, fork over 60% of your commissions, and let the agency pay for your rent and support functions.

Let's now look at the prospects for having your office at home. In addition to saving the monthly office rent, there are a few other advantages to having your office at home:

» The average person spends an hour each day commuting to and from work. You can use this extra hour to build your business instead of commuting. Over the course of a year you will have put over 200 extra hours into your business. This could equate to an extra placement or two.

» By working at home, you can make yourself available during more hours of the day. When you go to an office, you generally work from eight or 9 A.M. to 5 P.M. to coincide with the work cycle of others. Before eight and after five, anyone trying to talk with you will reach the community receptionist or your answering machine. Many candidates are only available before and after regular working hours.

Obviously, a recruiter renting an office can overcome the advantages of working at home by arriving earlier and staying later. Less obvious is how the home worker can overcome the advantages of renting an office. To explore this, let's take another look at the advantages of renting an office.

1. Having a receptionist to answer the phone and greet visitors is one of the more important features of a rented office, particularly if you want to project a professional image. Most recruiters working at home overcome this problem in one of two ways. They can install two phones, one for outgoing and the other one for incoming calls. With two phones, no one will get a busy signal when trying to call you. Many recruiters use an automatic switching device on their phone

that transfers the caller to an answering machine if the phone is in use. Personally, I hate leaving messages on answering machines and assume that others hate it, too, but many recruiters have no problem with answering machines. You can compensate for a receptionist through good scheduling and some imagination. Most clients are more than happy to meet at their place of business. However, if a client needs to meet with you outside the office, you can rent a conference room or invite your client to lunch and conduct your business over a good, tax deductible meal. Almost all your candidates will want to meet with you outside their workplace. Most recruiters have a favorite restaurant where they can meet a candidate for a cup of coffee. You are not expected to buy meals for candidates unless your business is entirely candidate driven (that is, search assignments are easy to land and candidates are worth their weight in gold). I've also gone to lunch with many candidates Dutch treat.

2. We've already addressed the issue of conference rooms. Having interview rooms in a nice setting depends on the value you place on personal contacts with clients and candidates. I meet both clients and candidates around the dining room table in my home, but I also severely limit the number of person-to-person contacts I make these days. Some recruiters run successful businesses almost entirely by phone, with only occasional personal contacts in a restaurant. Other recruiters who have been in business for years still maintain frequent personal contacts. Many options are available to you. Go with whatever makes you feel the most comfortable. Certainly, extensive per-

sonal contacts in the early stages of your business is probably beneficial, but these can take place in any quiet restaurant.

3. Having access to a copier and fax machine are now an essential part of the recruiting business. You'll be copying fee agreement letters and other correspondence and copying and faxing resumés. Having such equipment just down the hall from your rented office can be a wonderful convenience. However, there is a proliferation of businesses that supply these services to the general public. They probably charge no more for these services than the office rental people charge for using their equipment. If you happen to have a computer at home, you can get a modem with a fax attachment for under $100.

4. If you cannot do your own correspondence, secretarial services are available in most areas and charge no more than would the professional typist in an office cluster. The only advantage to the services offered by the office rental people is convenience. You may have to drive several blocks for these services if you work at home. Scheduling becomes important if you work at home. You don't want to be away from the phone during critical times of the day.

5. A rented office obviously gives your business a more professional appearance, which could be important if you plan a significant amount of personal contact with clients and candidates. You'll also have a more prestigious address to print on your stationary and business cards. Meeting with clients and candidates in plush surroundings might also be essential to your own self esteem. In the recruiting business, self confidence is an important factor in your success.

6. With an office to go to each morning, you are more likely to get up, dress nicely and go to work. Paying a substantial rent is a strong incentive for attending to business. An office at home is less apt to promote such good work habits, so you'll have to discipline yourself. A home office can only be successful if it is separated from the rest of the home. If this room is set aside only for work, you *will* work. If you allow other activities to take place there, your work will suffer.

7. To be a successful recruiter, you must put in eight solid hours of work each day. When you work in a rented office, you are there to work. There are no distractions. At home there can be hundreds of distractions. Not everyone has the mental tenacity to ignore other family members, neighbors or a favorite television program. Self discipline comes much easier in a rented office.

8. Working at home can sometimes be lonesome. You can get depressed when a big deal falls through or things are not happening in the way you expected. Being able to talk with other small business people who have undergone the same ordeal can be great therapy. If you are working at home, make it a point to get acquainted with other independent recruiters in your area. They can provide the same therapy via telephone, and they will have a greater understanding of what you are going through because they are in the same business.

Supplies

In addition to good communication skills, recruiting also involves the gathering, storing and dissemination of accurate information. Failure to obtain accurate information can lead to poor communication and, if compounded, to failure. Your function is to gather all the right information, record it, understand it, store it and use it appropriately.

You already have the forms you'll need to gather the right information. What you don't yet have is a method of storing and accessing it easily. You can do this with a card file system.

For maintaining client files, I suggest five-by-seven-inch file cards. A five-by-seven card will provide room to maintain vital information about a company on one side and the results of your contacts with the company on the other side of the card. You can use the cards to set up a convenient call-back system. Instead of going through all your client files every day to determine who you are scheduled to call back, set up a follow-up file using tab separators. Store your cards in a file box like the one used for separating recipes. Label the tabs with the months of the year. Label another set of tabs one to thirty-one for the dates of the current month. When you have the file properly set up, you should have twelve month tabs and thirty-one date tabs. To use the file, just place the client card behind the appropriate tab. For instance, if you promised to call back the XYZ company on August 20th to discuss a search assignment, you'd make that notation on the back of the XYZ client card and then file the card in your follow-up file under the month of August. When the first day of August rolls around, sort all the client cards you filed for follow-up in the month of August. The XYZ client card would be then be placed in the file marked 20th. On August 20th, you'll find the XYZ client card with your notation to call them back about a search assignment.

Candidate information should be stored in a separate file folder with the candidate's name on the tab. The file folders of all candidates should be filed alphabetically. The file folder might contain the candidate's resumé, the sheets you filled out when you interviewed him or her, references and other information about the candidate. In addition, it's a good idea to have the candidate listed on a three-by-five-inch file card. The cards can then be sorted by various categories so you don't need to pull a candidate's file each time you get a new search assignment. For instance, if you are working with salespeople, it might be convenient to sort your three by five candidate file cards by the type of product they sell or by the industry to which they sell. When you have 300 candidates in your database, it is much easier to go to the three by five file cards and look under widgets to find out who has widget-selling experience rather than going through 300 files.

One of your biggest expenses will be the printing of your stationary and business cards. Depending upon the quality of paper and the number of colors you use, it can cost between $150. and $400. for 500 copies of each item. The rest of your supplies will cost very little. Pencils, pens, paper clips, file folders, and other standard office items shouldn't break the bank.

Equipment

Eventually, you'll need a file cabinet. As your business grows, you'll need a place to store candidate files, completed search assignments, copies of correspondence, and business-related material. You'll also need a desk, although a table can substitute if it's not also used for another activity. Recruiting is a paper-intensive business that does not lend itself to being tidied up every day. Whatever you use as a desk should be devoted only to recruiting.

If you work at home, I recommend you get an electronic typewriter with memory. You can function very effectively by designing four or five form letters and placing them in the typewriter's memory. Each time you want to send out one of these letters, you need only type in the date and address of the selected boilerplate. The typewriter will do the rest automatically. Farming out your typing to a secretarial service can get expensive after awhile. If you must use a secretarial service, find one that has the capacity to store form letters. When you need a form letter sent out, the secretarial service will only have to type the date and address on the letter. This is a considerably less expensive than typing a new letter each time. You may have to spend two or three hundred dollars for a good secondhand typewriter, but you will get your money back in a few months with the money you save on secretarial services.

Your best bet, if you have the money, is a computer with a printer. I purchased a more than adequate computer and printer for around $1500. The computer stores and sorts all the information I need relating to clients, candidates, search assignments, and correspondence, and also stores a great many form letters that can be printed out with a few keystrokes. Because the recruiting business is an information business, a computer fits the business very well.

Obviously, the most important piece of equipment for your business is a telephone. If you have a phone in your home, you should get a second business phone installed. You can use the business phone for incoming calls and your regular phone for outgoing calls, or you can use just your business phone with call waiting or an answering machine to handle incoming calls. Don't try to conduct your recruiting business on your home phone. It just doesn't work well.

If you rent an office, you'll need to purchase the same basic equipment and supplies. However, since you are going to be in a much more professional setting, you will spend more on equipment. For example, you wouldn't want to use an old kitchen table as a desk in an office setting.

Your Budget

Go into any business with your eyes wide open. Look at your start-up costs and your monthly budget realistically. Although expenses will vary from area to area, here is what you'll need to conduct business at the most basic level, assuming that you will be working at home.

Initial Costs

Licenses, etc.	$	40.00
Phone (purchase and install)		125.00
Office supplies		50.00
Stationary		200.00
Typewriter		300.00
	Total	$715.00

Monthly Operating Costs

Phone bill		$400.00
Copying and faxing		40.00
Postage		20.00
Advertisement		100.00
Entertainment (clients & cand.)		60.00
	Total	$620.00

Your budget will vary, depending upon the equipment and the services (for example, secretarial services) you purchase, but what other business can you get into for so little money?

If you have small children, you will need daycare while you are working. Don't put yourself in the position of having to leave a client hanging while you attend to a demanding child. Clients have very little sympathy for what they might consider unprofessional behavior. They are professional and expect you to be professional as well. If you've decided to go into this business so you can stay home and take care of the kids, you're going to be disappointed. Recruiting demands your undivided attention.

Business Requirements

Most states require that you file a "fictitious name" document with your city or county. You are also required to get a business license in most places. A quick stroll through the government section of your local phone book and two or three phone calls will tell you exactly what is required of you.

You may wish to get an Employer Identification Number through the Internal Revenue Service. The EIN enables a client to inform the IRS of any payments made to your company. You can also use your Social Security number when a client needs your identification number, but if you ever hire anyone, an Employer Identification Number is required.

There are tax benefits associated with operating a business out of your home. When income tax time rolls around, It will be well worth the money to purchase a book that discusses the tax advantages of operating a home business.

I've tried to cover a great deal of territory in these few pages. Read this book over and over again until everything becomes second nature to you. While recruiting is a business where you will constantly learn new things, this book should serve as a foundation upon which to build your knowledge and your financial security.

In time, you will find your own way of doing the things taught in this book. That is as it should be. Just remember the basic rules. Every time you ignore or forget the basics, you lose a little. But that's enough talk about losing. The time has come for winning.

And celebrating!

Welcome to the world of recruiting!

CHAPTER 12

DOING BUSINESS ON THE INTERNET

Those who've explored the Internet know that there's a vast harvest of information in cyberspace just waiting to be plucked by the enterprising recruiter. A quick search of the "Personnel Wanted" and "Job Wanted" Web sites reveals hundreds of companies that are looking for thousands of employees, and thousands of people looking for new jobs.

And why not? In most cases, people can post their résumé on these sites for free. It's just like fishing: you cast your résumé into an international pool of applicants, and you never can tell when just the right company will come along, with just the right position, and discover you. It costs people nothing to fish this way, and the potential reward can be great.

By the same token, companies find posting their hiring needs on the Internet a tempting proposition. It may cost them a few bucks to advertise an opening on these Web sites, but it's a fraction of the cost of paying a recruiter and, in many instances, costs less then advertising in the local newspaper. Why not take the gamble? Maybe the odds of hiring a good employee aren't nearly as good as when using a recruiter, but if they hit the jackpot, they've saved a bundle in recruiting fees. At least, it seems that way on the surface. When it comes to employer/employee advertising, the Internet is like the advertising section of a gigantic newspaper that covers the entire world.

DOES IT WORK?

Few, if any, statistics are available that can tell you just how successful a company might be in finding personnel through the Internet. However, an examination of the system will give you many clues. For instance, a company in Boston looking for an accountant may find searching the Internet a waste of time. Plenty of good accountant résumés are posted on many Web sites, but they're from accountants all over the country, many of them just fishing for that "right" opportunity. Why deal with an accountant in New York or Los Angeles when there are plenty of good accountants in Boston?

Nationwide searches immediately expose the company to three very critical problems:

The first comes with arranging the needed interviews. Bringing a candidate from New York or Los Angeles to Boston can be quite expensive. In addition to airplane fares, there's the cost of the hotel and meals during the candidate's stay. Few candidates are willing to pay these expenses, so the costs generally fall upon the company. Obviously, the company would like to look at more than one candidate, so recruiting nationwide can become very costly.

The second problem arises when the company finds what appears to be a promising candidate. It costs a bundle to hire a candidate from another part of the country (see problem three below), so it's essential that the company be able to verify that this person is indeed a quality candidate. However, when all of the candidate's employment experience has taken place 2000 miles away, it's difficult to receive dependable reference information and employment verification. Why take such a gamble when there are good candidates locally?

The third problem comes when the company makes an offer and the candidate accepts the position. Moving a candidate from one city to another can be very expensive. The company might be moving a single person with a one-bedroom apartment, or it might be moving a six-person family with a four-bedroom house. It's not uncommon for a candidate to own the house where he or she is currently living. What sort of responsibility does the company have to help the candidate sell the house in Los Angeles and find a new one in Boston? Who pays if the candidate must sell the house at a loss? All these factors must be considered and negotiated before any deal can be closed.

There are, however, times when a company can use the Internet to great advantage in its search for good employees. Should this same Boston company need a sales representative in Los Angeles, it makes good sense to find a candidate currently living in the LA area. When a good candidate is located, the company's district manager can interview the candidate right there in Los Angeles—and the three problems previously cited all disappear.

THE INTERNET AND THE PROFESSIONAL RECRUITER

For the professional recruiter, the Internet is a mixed bag: used properly, it can be an asset; used improperly, it can quickly put you out of business.

First, let's look at how to use the Internet to put yourself out of business. The Internet is a very seductive mistress, tempting you to explore all the many Web sites where candidates post their résumés and where companies post "Help Wanted" notices. It looks like a cornucopia of candidates and job orders. However, the moment you view any of the résumés posted on these sites as candidates, or view any of the "Help Wanted" postings as job orders, you're starting on a downward spiral. These Web sites offer you value only if they do not influence you to abandon your expertise as a recruiter.

On one such Web site, you may occasionally find a candidate who lives in your local recruiting area. If that candidate has experience in your area of specialization, he or she should be recruited. That person may be a source of additional candidates and search assignments. Also, you may find a company in your area that's new to you and that hires people in your area of specialization. It's always nice to expand the marketplace for your candidates. Having said that, I caution you not to spend too much time looking at these Web sites; the searches can be time consuming and the payoff slim.

THE REAL RISKS

Whenever you're tempted to contact a company outside your recruiting area because they are looking for candidates you have in your database, remember the following:

1) The very best you can hope for is a one-in-fifty chance of making the placement. (See page 12, "Evaluating A Search Assignment.")

2) You'll be dealing with a client located outside your recruiting area, and you'll have no candidates living in the client's area.

3) Even if you get one of your candidates interested in relocating, you must deal with the interviewing and relocation problems discussed previously. This isn't where you want to be spending your time.

Should you become inspired to recruit candidates from other areas of the country for your out-of-town client, remember: Your client has access to the same Internet sites as you have. Your chances of placing an out-of-area candidate with an out-of area-client are less than 1 percent.

The real threat these Web sites pose to your career, however, isn't quite so obvious. Web sites can lull you into believing that there's an easier and more lucrative way to make money recruiting. Should you fall prey to such thinking, your days as a recruiter are numbered. This kind of thinking will destroy your good work habits and set you on the road to becoming an employment agency with an income that never exceeds twenty-five thousand dollars per year.

USING THE INTERNET PROPERLY

The Internet can play a definitive role in helping you become a more successful recruiter. You can have your own domain site on the Internet for $25 per month or less. Used properly, this inexpensive site can have a considerable impact on your business.

If you've never had your own Web site and are not sure how to proceed, there's a lot of help out there. Nowadays, almost every ISP (Internet Service Provider) offers its clients space for their own Web sites and will "host" them free of charge. Most offer you up to six megabytes of free space, and if you need more, you can purchase it for a nominal fee.

The drawback to using an ISP to "host" your Web site is the URL address you're stuck with. If your ISP is Prodigy, for instance, your URL address is going to read http://www.prodigy.page/yoursite.com* However, if you purchase space from an independent host, your URL will be just http://www.yoursite.com. Since almost every URL begins with http://www., anyone wanting to reach your site need only remember or type in yoursite.com to find the location of your Web site. It might we worth that extra $20 per month to have a simple URL address for your site. We'll talk more about locating and designing your Web site later.

THE PURPOSE OF
AN INTERNET SITE

Before planning your Web site you must have certain specific goals in mind:

First, you want a site that entices your clients to look to you for the candidates you specialize

---

* I've used "yoursite.com" as the domain name for your Internet site as an example only. We'll discuss finding the proper domain name for your site a little later. You will, of course, use your assigned domain name rather than "yoursite" for your actual URL address.

in before looking anywhere else.

Secondly, you want a site that encourages candidates to look to you first for help in finding a new position.

FOR YOUR CLIENTS

To accomplish the first objective, you must have a Web site that offers your clients immediate access to a smorgasbord of good, qualified candidates. For example, if accountants are your area of specialization, you want to make it *very* convenient for your client to go to your Web site and find precisely the accountant they're looking for. So convenient, in fact, that they'll look at your Web site before doing anything else about searching for the right candidate. That's one reason for having a very simple URL address. More important, however, is to have a Web site that the client will feel comfortable using.

Keep it simple. Many Web sites, in an effort to dazzle the visitor with all their wonderful technology, make finding anything on the site difficult. You know exactly why your client is visiting your site. They're looking for a candidate. Help them find that candidate by making things as simple as possible.

Your home page should identify your Web site with a very simple banner and, without requiring people to scroll down the page, offer them an easy first choice.

I am looking for a:
general accountant
cost accountant
accounts receivable account
accounts payable account

account manager
assistant comptroller
comptroller
(others)—you get the drift.

Your client need only click on the candidate area of his choice to have access to all the candidates you've posted. Yes. I know I've harped about how meaningless titles are, but clients still use them, so you must adapt to their style of candidate searching. The client's next option might be with regard to length of experience.

I want someone with:
Entry level experience
1–2 years' experience
2–4 years' experience
More than 4 years' experience

There are a number of other options you might offer your clients, such as the types of software packages the candidate must be familiar with. However, each option narrows the search and eliminates all candidates outside that particular search parameter. You don't want them eliminating too many candidates, and the more options you offer, the less candidates they'll end up with. Obviously, if you specialize in programmers, the programming language is of paramount importance and should be offered as a choice. However, if the client asks only for candidates with experience working with and/or modifying ZLA software, they may eliminate too many good candidates. You might not want to offer them such a screening tool.

You may want to offer your clients different screening methods to see which ones work best for them. Don't be afraid to ask them about their preferences. You'll be demonstrating your site in order to market it, so there'll be ample opportunity to solicit their opinions.

Assuming that the client has indicated that he or she is looking for a general accountant with two to four years' experience, the client will be provided a list of candidates from your database who have that background. The list might look something like this:

Candidates meeting your specifications:
Candidate 0043
Candidate 0021
Candidate 0133
Candidate 0078

The candidates should be listed as numbers or letters that you can easily identify. For example, candidate 0043 might be John Dillinger.

Your client then clicks on the candidate and receives a synopsis of that candidate's background and experience. This synopsis shouldn't be a complete résumé, but it should provide enough information to stimulate the client's interest in pursuing the candidate.

A good synopsis might be:

John (use the candidate's first name rather than a number—it personalizes the individual) graduated from USC in June 1999 with a degree in accounting, and has been working for the same company since then. The company John works for has average annual sales of $200 million, and uses PRQ and XYZ software as its primary accounting packages. However, John has also been exposed to DRL software at work, and studied LMN software in school. In addition to general ledger accounting, John has worked in both accounts receivable and accounts payable, and has experience with inventory control and cost accounting.

John works on a team with direct responsibility for the R&D and personnel departments. As a member of that team, he has also been exposed to shipping, receiving, and most other accounting areas of the company, because it is required that all team members become familiar with the entire accounting system. The company John works for is currently downsizing, which limits his potential growth. John is looking for an aggressive company that appreciates an energetic employee who enjoys new learning experiences. (If you have references for John, add pertinent information.) John's co-workers say that he is reliable, cooperative, intelligent, and progressive in his thinking. They feel he would be a great asset to any accounting department.

AN EASY PLACEMENT?

Your goal, obviously, is to get the client to call you for more information about John. However, there may be times when a client selects a candidate who would not be interested in the company the client represents, or a candidate who has just accepted another position. Therefore, it's important that you have at your fingertips several similar candidates to offer the client. This not only gives you the opportunity to set up an interview between John and client, but provides an opportunity to pitch other candidates as well.

"If you like John's background and experience, you're going to love Jane. It sounds like you're looking for someone who can... Jane would be ideal for such a position."

Your goal, naturally, is to place a candidate with this company, which is best done by increasing the odds of your getting the placement to 80 percent. The client called you; the client likes your candidate(s). You need only persuade the client that the entire process can be completed in one easy afternoon by interviewing four or five of your best candidates and picking the best one. (If you've forgotten how to do this, go back and reread pages 12–15.)

Wouldn't it be wonderful if every company that employs the candidates you specialize in looked at your Web site before making any other recruiting efforts? Make it a friendly site that's very simple to navigate around and they just might. Most people looking for new employees are going to take the path of least resistance. If your Internet site offers the client this path, they will take it.

MARKETING YOUR WEB SITE TO CLIENTS

Obviously, no client is going to use your Web site if they don't know it's there or they don't know how to access it. Therefore, your biggest job will be teaching the proper person(s) in each client company how to locate your site. For Internet-savvy people, this can be done over the phone. However, it's best if you can make an appointment to meet with them.

Every ISP offers its clients a place where they can store the URL addresses of their favorite Web sites. You want your clients to store your Web address as one of their favorites. Wouldn't it be grand if all the client had to do was to look under their favorite Web sites, click on "Accountants," and your Web site came up?

This is very easily accomplished. Using the client's computer, all you have to do is open up your Internet site using your URL address. Once your home page is open, you need only

160

click on the bar where is says "Favorites" and then click on "Save this page." The URL address for your Web site has been stored with the client's other favorite Web sites under the heading you choose—such as "Accountants."

However, this should be done only after you've given the client a demonstration of how your Web site will work for them. Walk them through the site once and then have them try it. Have them use it several times in your presence until you're sure they're comfortable with using it. Teach them how to download or print out the synopsis for each candidate they're interested in. Regardless of how comfortable someone is in using the Internet, they like to have a "hard" copy in hand when they find a candidate they like. When you feel that they're using the site comfortably, place your URL in their "Favorite" column as discussed above. Show them how to click on "Accountants" to reach your site. Have them try it once or twice. Never assume they are so computer savvy that they don't need this instruction.

Before leaving, assure them that you want to make the site as convenient for them as possible. Ask them to try it a few times and note any ideas they can think of that might make it easier for them to use.

Should you discover, at some future date, that they were looking for an accountant and didn't use your Web site, don't hesitate to call them to learn why. You'll never overcome their objections to using your site if you don't know what the problem is.

FOR YOUR CANDIDATES

The Internet site you've developed for your clients can be equally attractive to your candidates. It offers them exposure to the entire market place without letting anyone know they're looking. They must, however, feel comfortable that your synopsis of their background and experience does not divulge who they are. Their current employer may be using your site to look for new employees, and candidates cannot afford to let their employers know they're "looking." Therefore, it's wise to let them review and comment on your synopsis of them before posting it. They'll be much more interested in becoming a part of your candidate database if they can participate in how you present them to your clients.

The client Web site can be a great recruiting tool for candidates as well. Almost all candidates have some "reason for leaving" their current position. It may be a commute problem, an unfriendly co-worker, or a lack of advancement possibilities. (See page 84 for the section on "reason for leaving.") Once you've recruited a candidate, you and the candidate can put together a synopsis that satisfies that candidate's "reason for leaving."

Some recruiters put up a separate Web site for candidates, in which they list various job openings. However, I don't recommend this for several reasons:

1) Candidates who don't fit the position are going to see the listing and want the job. You don't want candidates who are actively looking to call and ask you why you haven't represented them to the company.

2) Trying to market the site to all eligible candidates will be a nightmare and won't pay for the time spent marketing it. Can you imagine trying to contact all the accountants in your area and showing them how to access the site?

3) Undesirable candidates are going to discover the site and want to be represented. They will take up your time and space. Further, if they don't find their synopsis represented on the client's Web site, they are going to trouble you. It's easier to reject unwanted candidates if you're not inadvertently advertising for them.

4) They might be able to figure out who your client is and represent themselves to the client, leaving you out of the picture. You'll not only lose a candidate but also a search assignment.

DESIGNING AND UPLOADING YOUR WEB SITE ON THE INTERNET

At one time, only computer professionals had the knowledge and abilities to design and upload a Web site onto the Internet. However, this is no longer true. Many ISPs not only provide you with free space for your Web site but also provide you with simple tools for putting one together. There are also many Web sites that will happily teach you how to design a site or how to program in *html* or *Java,* the principal languages found on all Web sites. There are also many sites that allow you to download the software you need in order to upload your Web site once you've designed it.

However, designing and programming a Web site, even with all this help, can be time consuming. While I have programmed and uploaded several Web sites, I firmly believe

that a recruiter's time is better spent recruiting. Therefore, I recommend hiring someone to do it for you. Be sure, however, that you're in control and completely involved in the design of the site, so that it functions the way you want it to. Make sure you have an opportunity to test it several times before it's uploaded to the host site. If you've had very little experience with the Internet, or with computers, be sure to get instruction in how Web sites are put together, so that your ideas are compatible with the way computers function.

One of the most interesting features of your Web site is that it will be constantly changing. You'll continually add new candidates to the site and remove old candidates. You don't want to be placed in a position where you have to rehire the professional every time you need to make such a change. Therefore, be sure your Web site is set up so that you can add and remove candidates as need arises.

Whenever you have a new candidate, you need to be able to write a synopsis of that candidate's background and then put it in the appropriate place on your Web site. For instance, if the client is looking for a general accountant with two to four years' experience, you want to be sure that all candidates with that background appear when the client does a search. Therefore, your Web site must contain a simple mechanism for you to add, remove, or change a candidate's synopsis as necessary to keep it current.

SELECTING A DOMAIN NAME

I mentioned earlier that you'd have a domain name that becomes the main part of your

URL address. In order to assure that everyone has their own private URL address, all domain sites must be purchased and registered so that no one else can use the same address. For example, *Discover* magazine owns the domain name discover.com, and anyone can access their Web site just by just typing in "www.discover. com." Obviously, many people would like to own the domain site discover.com, but *Discover* magazine got there first. No one else can use that domain name.

If you were recruiting accountants, you'd probably want to have a domain name like accountants.com. Unfortunately, that name, as well as many similar names, is already taken. Therefore, you're going to have to do some searching and use your imagination to come up with an appropriate domain name that's not already in use. The best way to find a domain name is to get on the Internet and visit some of the Web sites that will tell you whether a name has been taken and, if it hasn't, will help you register the name you've chosen. You can find many such sites by using any of the popular search engines and typing in "domain names."

Most people who pay attention to the Internet know that the most popular ending for a domain name is .com, as in discover.com or usedcars.com. As a result, most of the decent .com names are in use. They're also the most expensive. However, there are many other endings available that aren't as well known and are thus not as expensive or already taken. In fact, several new endings will be available near the end of year 2001. Owning accountants.viz isn't such a bad domain site to have after all.

ABOUT THE AUTHOR

Richard Mackie began his professional career as an inspector with the San Diego County Department of Agriculture after receiving an M.S. Degree from the University of Idaho in 1957. After 18 disillusioning months enforcing the state's agricultural code, he accepted a position as Public Health Entomologist with the San Diego County Department of Public Health. He published articles in various professional journals, wrote legislation, and was promoted to head a public health agency.

In 1976 he was appointed Chief Public Health Officer. In addition to frequent speaking and public television engagements, he attended international conferences sponsored by the World Health Organization. Three years later, disgusted with government bureaucracy, he decided to explore the entrepreneurial world. For the next two years he worked as a management consultant. Although consulting was fun, the constant moving was not. Settling in the San Francisco Bay Area, he found, at the age of forty-eight, that his priorities had changed. He needed a profession that would pay well but would also allow him to work where and when he wanted.

After trying several disappointing enterprises that "guaranteed" to make him rich and "guaranteed" to let him be his own boss, he discovered recruiting. It seemed to respond to all his goals. He had the option of working for someone else or of working alone at home. He could learn a skill that was in constant demand.   He could control his income by working at a specific pace and by working smart. He entered the profession, however, with a good deal of apprehension. He had heard about "head hunters," had fought dishonesty in government, and was not interested in dealing with deception in private enterprise. However, he soon discovered that any recruiter who was not totally honest with himself, his clients and his candidates would soon end up in the scrap heap. He found it was not a business that would tolerate deception. At last, he had found a business that would allow him to function with integrity.

In his first year of recruiting he made almost $120,000 in sales, pocketing just over $50,000 for himself and making about $70,000 for his company. By the end of that same year he found himself teaching the art of successful recruiting to others and thoroughly enjoying it. For the next seven to eight years he continued to teach recruiting while maintaining his own recruiting business.

While he enjoyed teaching recruiting, he did not enjoy sharing over one half of his income with the agency where he worked. Therefore, in July of 1991, he moved his business to his home. He discovered that he could work part time at home and still make more money then by working full time for an agency and giving 55 or 60 percent of his income away.

Working at home, however, deprived him of the chance to teach recruiting. He missed watching eager employees take the day's lesson to their desks to try it out. He missed seeing the light of discovery blink on as pupils discovered that the lesson worked the way the teacher had said it would. Looking over the teaching materials he had accumulated through the years, he felt they were too valuable to waste. It was time he shared his recruiting "secrets" with the world rather than with just a few students at a time. Take This Job & Sell It! evolved from those lessons.

Richard Mackie believes there is a pressing need for our country to change the way people work. "We need to get more people off the freeways and working at home. We also need to make the process of hiring people more economical and successful for America's companies." Take This Job & Sell It! is dedicated to these ends.

GLOSSARY

Agency: Any company whose primary business is providing personnel to other businesses (clients).

Candidate: Any person with the proper skills and experience to fill a given position successfully. To be considered a real candidate, the person should also have some interest in the position being offered.

Client: Any person or company willing to pay you a fee to locate appropriate candidates to fill a position in their company.

Contingency Fee: A fee paid to a recruiter by a client on the condition that the recruiter find a candidate that the client hires. If the client does not hire the recruiter's candidate, the recruiter receives nothing, regardless of how much work the recruiter put into an attempt to fill the position.

Download: The transfer or copying of files or information from one computer to another, i.e., from your Web page to your client's computer.

Hiring Manager: The person who originates the search assignment. Most likely, the hiring manager has prepared the job description and is the person that the candidate will report to when hired. Most recruiters view the hiring manager as their real client.

Home page: The main page displayed when visiting a Web site. The home page usually provides a directory to sub-pages within the site.

Host: Any computer used to store information and Web sites on behalf of others.

Human Resources: The company personnel department, one small (and frequently disliked) function of which is to locate candidates for employment.

ISP (Internet Service Provider): A company that provides you with access to the Internet through their phone lines and computer sites.

Job Description: A summary of the duties and responsibilities of a company position, with specifications for skills needed by a candidate for that position.

Placement: The act of successfully filling a position for a client and collecting an appropriate fee for the service rendered.

Recruitment Agency: Any company whose primary business is finding candidates to fill permanent positions for client companies.

Search Assignment: A specific agreement between a recruiter or recruitment agency and a client company to find candidates to fill a particular position for a predetermined fee when the assignment is successfully completed.

Search Engine: A directory on the Internet where information on a subject can be located by entering specific "key" words that the engine will search for.

URL (Universal Resource Locator): is the address assigned to a Web site so that it can be located from anywhere in the world by simply typing in the address.

WWW (World Wide Web): An Internet service used for locating and browsing Internet resources.

INDEX

168

BOOKS & FORMS

Additional copies of *Take This Job & Sell It!* as well as multiple copies of the forms used in this book are available directly from the publisher. Credit card holders may order by fax or phone. Forms are available individually in packets of 100, in starter sets, and in recruiter sets. Prices and contents of forms are noted in the following table.

FORM NAME	NO. OF PAGES	STARTER SET CONTENTS	RECRUITER SET CONTENTS	INDIVIDUAL FORMS (100 EACH)
Search Assignment Form	3	2 sets	10 sets	$30
Marketing Worksheets	2	5 "	20 "	$20
Candidate File Card	1	5 "	20 "	$10
Client Record	1	5 "	20 "	$10
Candidate Agreement	1	2 "	10 "	$10
Company Organization	4	2 "	10 "	$40
Peer Reference	2	5 "	20 "	$20
Manager Reference	2	5 "	20 "	$20
Price		**$9.95**	**$39.95**	(as above)

Please send me:_____ Starter Set(s) @ $9.95   Recruiter Set(s) @ $39.95

Individual packets of the following forms:

_____ copies of *Take This Job and Sell It!* @ $24.95

There is no charge for shipping and handling, but if you'd like your order shipped UPS please add $3. California residents add 7.75% sales tax. Mail orders should be sent to **QED Press,** 155 Cypress Street, Fort Bragg, CA 95437. Credit Card holders may phone 1-800-773-7782 or (707) 964-9520 or fax (707) 964-7531 to place their orders.

Name_____

Address_____

City_____ State_____ Zip_____

Method of Payment:

❏ Check ❏ Money order ❏ VISA ❏ MasterCard ❏ Discover ❏ American Express

Credit card Number_____**Expiration** Date_____

Authorized Signature:_____